Hiking Big Bend National Park

Help Us Keep This Guide Up to Date

Every effort has been made by the author and editors to make this guide as accurate and use-ful as possible. However, many things can change after a guide is published—trails are rerouted, regulations change, techniques evolve, facilities come under new management, etc.

We would love to hear from you concerning your experiences with this guide and how you feel it could be improved and kept up to date. While we may not be able to respond to all comments and suggestions, we'll take them to heart, and we'll also make certain to share them with the author. Please send your comments and suggestions to the following address:

The Globe Pequot Press
Reader Response/Editorial Department
P.O. Box 480
Guilford, CT 06437

Or you may e-mail us at:

editorial@GlobePequot.com

Thanks for your input, and happy trails!

Hiking Big Bend National Park

Second Edition

Laurence Parent

With the assistance of Mary K. Manning and other hikers and writers of the Big Bend National Park staff

FALCONGUIDES®

GUILFORD, CONNECTICUT
HELENA, MONTANA
AN IMPRINT OF THE GLOBE PEQUOT PRESS

FALCONGUIDES®

All photographs are by Laurence Parent unless otherwise
noted.
Maps by XNR Productions, Inc. © Morris Book Publishing, LLC

Library of Congress Cataloging-in-Publication Data
Parent, Laurence.
   Hiking Big Bend National Park / by Laurence Parent ;
   with assistance from hikers and writers from the Big
   Bend National Park staff.
        p. cm.
   "A Falcon guide."
   Includes bibliograhical references.
   ISBN 978-0-7627-3142-8 (pbk.)
   1. Hiking –Texas–Big Bend National Park–Guidebooks.
   2. Big Bend National Park (Tex.)–Guidebooks. I. Title.
GV199.42.T492B547 1996
917.64'93–dc20
                                        96-12282

Manufactured in the United States of America
Second Edition/Fifth Printing

> To buy books in quantity for corporate use
> or incentives, call **(800) 962–0973**
> or e-mail **premiums@GlobePequot.com.**

Contents

Overview

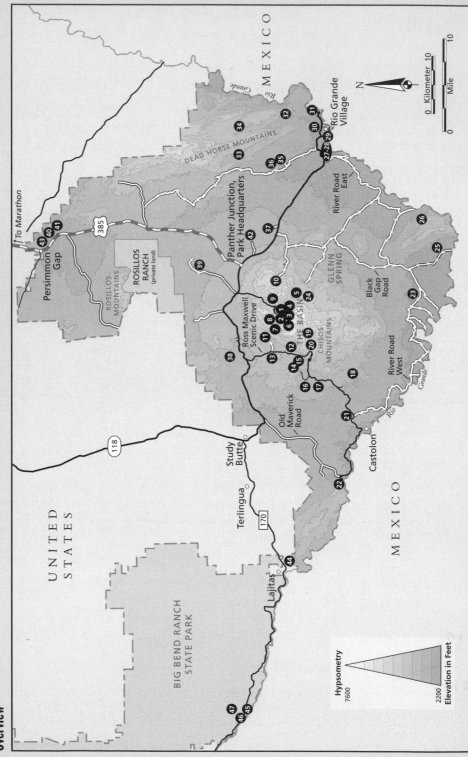

Acknowledgments

This book project was completed with the contributions of many people. Special thanks go to the members of the Big Bend National Park staff who hiked the majority of the park trails and wrote up the respective descriptions. These hikers and writers were Audrey Ashcraft, Karen Boucher, Don Corrick, Mark Flippo, John Forsythe, Mark Herberger, Mary K. Manning, Gus Sánchez, Jeff Selleck, Raymond Skiles, and Carol Sperling. David Alloway, formerly with the Texas Parks and Wildlife Department, did the same for the trails at Big Bend Ranch State Park. Mary K. Manning helped immensely with the revised edition.

Dennis Vásquez and Mary K. Manning did most project organization. I did most of the primary editing, but was assisted by Mary K. Manning, Valerie Naylor, and Dennis Vásquez. Fact-checking was done by several members of the Big Bend staff. Thanks also go to Carl Robinson of the Big Bend Natural History Association and Randall Green of Falcon Press for encouraging this project. I also wish to thank Earl Nottingham for assisting me on the hikes I did for this book.

The Rio Grande flows tranquilly above Hot Springs Canyon.

Introduction

For hikers and backpackers in Texas, Big Bend National Park is the state's number one destination. More than 1,200 square miles of undeveloped land beckon with endless miles of trails and cross-country routes. The park is not only the largest tract of public land in Texas but is also one of the best examples of Chihuahuan Desert in the country.

The Chihuahuan Desert sprawls across a vast expanse of northern Mexico, West Texas, and southern New Mexico. Like other deserts, it is defined as an area of low precipitation, generally less than 10 inches per year at lower elevations. Specific plant communities and climate patterns differentiate the Chihuahuan Desert from other deserts. One plant in particular, the lechuguilla, is unique to the Chihuahuan Desert. The plant, growing in a green rosette of thick, fibrous leaves tipped with wicked spines, quickly makes itself apparent to unwary hikers at Big Bend.

Like islands in a sea, rugged mountain ranges dot the vast lowland expanses of the Chihuahuan Desert. Some of these mountains, such as the Chisos Mountains at Big Bend, reach high enough elevations to attract additional rainfall. The additional rain and cooler temperatures allow forests to grow on the upper slopes of these ranges. A forest of pinyon pine, juniper, and oak cloaks the Chisos Mountains; bigger ranges, such as the Sierra del Carmen across the river from the park in Mexico, contain lush forests of Arizona pine, Douglas-fir, aspen, and other trees.

Water is of paramount importance in the desert country of Big Bend National Park. Plants adapt to the hot, dry terrain by growing small leaves. Waxy coatings limit transpiration of water by plants. Cacti have done away with leaves altogether. Plants such as the ocotillo only produce leaves after sufficient rainfall. Seeds of many annuals will not even germinate in dry years; when they do germinate, they develop, flower, and fruit quickly, before the moisture disappears. Animals also adapt to the arid conditions. Most come out to feed and hunt only at night during cooler temperatures. The kangaroo rat never has to drink at all; it obtains water from its food.

Because water is scarce at Big Bend, springs and water holes are particularly valuable. Permanent creeks are rare. One major exception, the Rio Grande, creates a long, narrow oasis, a ribbon of green along the southern boundary of the park. The river and springs are vital to the park's wildlife.

The many trails at Big Bend National Park visit some of these springs and the deep canyons of the Rio Grande. They wander through the high, wooded peaks of the Chisos Mountains and past the ruins of old ranches and settlements. This guide will help take you to many places that park visitors unwilling to leave their cars will never see. Some of the most spectacular scenery in Texas awaits you.

Backcountry Ethics

A few simple rules and courtesies will help preserve the natural environment and allow others to enjoy their outdoor experience. Every hiker has at least a slight impact on the land and other visitors. Your goal should be to minimize that impact. Some of the rules and suggestions may seem overly restrictive and confining; however, with increasing use of the park, such rules have become more necessary. All can be followed with little inconvenience and will contribute to a better outdoor experience for you and others.

Camping

Three developed campgrounds lie within the park, at the Basin, Rio Grande Village, and Castolon. Showers can be found at Rio Grande Village. Several primitive car campsites are found along the park's back roads. Hikers have innumerable options for backcountry camping. Within the popular Chisos Mountains, backpackers must use designated sites scattered throughout the high country. A free permit must be obtained at Panther Junction or the Basin visitor center ahead of time. During busy times, such as Thanksgiving, Christmas, and college spring break, it may be difficult to obtain a site in the mountains. Within certain guidelines, most of the rest of the park is open to backcountry camping. As with the Chisos Mountains, a free permit must be obtained, but you are not restricted to specific sites.

Camp at least 100 yards away from water sources. The vegetation at creeks and springs is often the most fragile. Camping well away prevents trampling and destruction of plant life. Destruction of vegetation usually leads to erosion and muddying of water sources. Additionally, camping 100 yards away prevents runoff of wash water, food scraps, and human waste into the water supply. In desert areas, a spring may be the only water source for miles. If you camp too close, you may keep wildlife from reaching vital water. Dry camps have advantages—they are usually warmer and have fewer insects.

Pick a level site that won't require modification to be usable. Don't destroy vegetation as you set up camp. The ideal camp is probably on bare desert ground in the lower areas of the park. Don't trench around the tent site; choose a site with good natural drainage. If possible, pick a site that has already been used so that you won't trample another. If you remove rocks, sticks, or other debris, replace them when you depart. You want to leave no trace of your visit when you leave.

Be courteous—don't pitch your tent right next to other people's camp. Remember, they are probably out in the backcountry to get away from crowds, too. For similar reasons, avoid creating excessive noise. Camp must be set up at least 100 yards away from the trail and, ideally, out of sight.

Carry out all of your trash, including cigarette butts. Food containers are much lighter once the contents have been consumed and are easy to carry. Improve the area for future visitors and take out trash that others have left behind.

When available, such as in the high Chisos Mountains, use backcountry toilets. Otherwise, dig a 6- to 8-inch-deep hole as far away from water, campsites, and trails as possible and bury human wastes. Carry out toilet paper along with the rest of your trash.

Because wood is scarce in desert country, fires are prohibited. In addition, wildfires can start easily in the dry terrain and campfires leave scars that are slow to heal. For cooking purposes, backpacking stoves are much easier, quicker, and more efficient.

A few areas are closed to backcountry camping, including any sites within 0.5 mile of a road, a developed area, the Mariscal Mine, or Hot Springs. Also, don't camp within 100 yards of a historical or an archaeological site. Common sense dictates that you don't camp near a cliff edge or in a dry, flood-prone wash. Within the Chisos Mountains, several areas are closed to campers: the Basin and the north section of the Chisos Mountains, including the area along the Lost Mine Trail, Pine Canyon, Green Gulch, and the high ridge that includes Pulliam and Vernon Bailey Peaks. Two other restricted areas include the part of Burro Mesa that lies above 3,400 feet in elevation and within 100 yards of any tinaja on Mesa de Anguila.

The Trail

Don't shortcut switchbacks on the trail. Switchbacks were built to ease the grade on climbs and to limit erosion. Shortcutting, although it may be shorter, usually takes more effort and causes erosion.

Always give horses and other pack animals the right of way. Stand well away from the trail and make no sudden movements or noises that could spook the animals. Motorized and mechanized vehicles, including mountain bikes, are prohibited on all park trails. Likewise, pets are not allowed because of their potential to disturb or threaten wildlife. There are no kennels in the park, so it's best to leave them at home if you plan to hike.

If you smoke, stop in a safe spot and make sure that cigarettes and matches are dead out before proceeding. Be sure to take your butts with you. Don't smoke in windy and dry conditions.

Don't do anything to disturb the natural environment. No hunting is allowed in the park. Don't cut trees or other plants. Resist the temptation to pick wildflowers. Don't blaze trees, carve initials on rocks, or add improvements to campsites. Don't remove any Indian relics or historic items. All such artifacts are protected by law in the park and are important to future visitors.

Rules and regulations can be boring and tedious, but they will help make sure that Big Bend National Park remains the gem that it is for future generations.

Safety

With preparation and good judgment, few mishaps should occur on your hikes. The following sections elaborate on some of the potential hazards that you may encounter on the trail. Don't let the list scare you; most mishaps are easily prevented.

Weather

More emergencies at Big Bend are probably related to weather than any other factor. Not surprisingly, heat causes many problems in the region, particularly from April to October. The desert heat can be brutal in summer. Shade temperatures of greater than 110 degrees Fahrenheit are not uncommon.

On your hikes, carry and drink adequate water. For long hikes in hot weather, plan to carry at least a gallon of water per person per day. Wear a broad-brimmed hat and use sunscreen. Even summer hikes in the Chisos Mountains will usually be quite warm, especially in May and June before the summer rains begin. If you do summer hikes in desert areas of the park, try to start early in the morning to avoid the worst of the heat. Don't push as hard, take frequent breaks, and carry lots of water. All but the shortest desert trails are best left for cooler times of the year.

Excessive heat and dehydration can cause many serious physical problems, from headaches and nausea to heart and kidney failure. A common effect is heat exhaustion. Symptoms of heat exhaustion include skin that is still moist and sweaty, but you may feel weak, dizzy, irritable, nauseated, or have muscle cramps. Find a cool, shady place to rest, drink plenty of liquids, and eat a few crackers or other source of salt. After you feel better, keep drinking plenty of liquids and limit physical activity. Hike out during a cooler time of day. The condition is not usually serious, but go to a doctor as soon as possible.

Heat stroke is less common, but can develop with prolonged exposure to very hot conditions. It occurs when the body's temperature regulation system stops functioning, resulting in a rapid rise in body temperature. The skin is hot, flushed, and bone-dry. Confusion and unconsciousness can quickly follow. Heat stroke is life-threatening. Immediately get the victim into the coolest available place. Remove excess clothes and dampen skin and remaining clothes with water. Fan the victim for additional cooling. If a cool stream or pond is nearby, consider immersing the victim. You must get the body temperature down quickly. Seek medical help immediately.

At the other temperature extreme, cold can also be a hazard at Big Bend. Even in the hot desert areas, sudden thunderstorms in late summer can drench you and, at the least, make you uncomfortably cool. In the Chisos Mountains, temperatures can plummet in storms. When combined with wet clothes or lack of shelter, such conditions can lead to hypothermia.

Hypothermia occurs when the body's internal temperature falls. If conditions turn wet and cold and a member of your party begins to slur speech, shiver constantly, or becomes clumsy, sleepy, or unreasonable, immediately get the hiker into shelter and out of wet clothes. Give the victim warm liquids to drink and get him into a sleeping bag with one or more people. Skin-to-skin contact conducts body heat to the victim most effectively. This is not a time for modesty; you may save the victim's life.

The weather at Big Bend is usually very temperate in winter, but fronts and storms can blow in quickly. Snow usually blankets the mountains at least a time or two every winter. During and after such storms, park temperatures can often fall well below freezing.

It's easy to prepare for most cold weather problems. Always take extra warm clothes, especially in winter, in the Chisos Mountains, and on extended hikes. Wool and some synthetics still retain some insulating capability when wet; cotton is worthless. Rain gear is essential, especially on hikes in the mountains in late summer and early fall. Carry a reliable tent on longer trips. Hole up and wait for the bad weather to pass, rather than attempting a long hike out. Most storms at Big Bend, especially in summer, are of short duration.

Temperature extremes are not the only weather-related hazard; lightning from storms poses another threat. When thunderstorms appear, seek lower ground. Stay off hilltops and away from lone trees and open areas. Lightning makes exposed mountain peaks and ridges especially hazardous. The most common thunderstorms at Big Bend develop in late summer afternoons. Plan to start your hikes early to reach the high peaks and ridges of the Chisos Mountains by lunchtime so that you can leave those areas before storms appear. If you get caught in a lightning storm, seek shelter in a low-lying grove of small, equal-size trees, if possible. Put down your metal-framed packs, tripods, and metal tent poles and move well away from them.

Although floods would not seem to be a threat in the desert terrain of Big Bend National Park, sudden downpours, especially in late summer, can turn a dry wash into a raging, muddy torrent in minutes. Stay out of narrow canyons boxed in by cliffs during heavy rains. Even though you may be in sunshine, watch the weather upstream from you. Camp well above and away from the Rio Grande. For evidence of the river's past floods, take a look at the high water mark on the wall of the bathroom at the Santa Elena Canyon parking area. The river is not even in sight, yet it rose enough to flood the parking area. In addition, never camp in that tempting sandy site in the bottom of a dry desert wash. Storms upstream from you can send water sweeping down desert washes with unbelievable fury.

Conditioning

Good physical conditioning will make your trip safer and much more pleasant. Do not push yourself too hard, especially on the steep, higher elevation trails of the Chisos Mountains. If you have been sedentary for a long time, consider getting a physical exam before starting hiking. Ease into hiking; start with the easy hikes and graduate to more difficult ones. This guide lists everything from short, barrier-free routes to rugged, multi-day backpacks. Pick a trail that fits your ability. Do not push your party any harder or faster than its weakest member can handle comfortably. Know your limits. When you get tired, rest or turn back. Remember, you are out here to have fun.

Be prepared for the hike. Read this guidebook and the specific hike description. Study maps and other books on the area. Carry all necessary equipment to ensure comfort and safety. Every effort has been made to create a guidebook that is as accurate and current as possible, but a few errors may still creep in. Additionally, roads and trails change. Signs can disappear, springs can dry up, roads can wash out, and trails can be rerouted. Talk to park rangers about current road and trail conditions and water sources. Check the weather forecast. Find out the abilities and desires of your hiking companions before hitting the trail.

Altitude

Only the Chisos Mountains attain a very high elevation in the park. Since the highest peak reaches only 7,825 feet, most people will have few breathing problems on any of the hikes in the park. At most, people coming from low elevations may have a little trouble in the higher reaches of the Chisos Mountains. Until you acclimatize, you may suffer from a little shortness of breath and tire more easily. A very few hikers may develop headaches, nausea, fatigue, or other mild symptoms such as swelling of the face, hands, ankles, or other body areas at the highest altitudes. Mild symptoms should not change your plans. Rest for a day or two to acclimate. Retreating a thousand feet or so will often clear up any symptoms. Spending several days at moderate altitude before climbing high will often prevent any problems.

The Chisos Mountains are not high enough to cause the serious symptoms of altitude sickness, such as pulmonary edema (fluid collecting in the lungs) or cerebral edema (fluid accumulating in the brain), except in very rare cases. Should these symptoms develop, immediately get the victim to lower elevations and medical attention.

Companions

Pick your hiking companions wisely. Consider their experience and physical and mental fitness. Try to form groups of relatively similar physical ability. Pick a leader, especially on long trips or with large groups. Ideally, have at least one experienced hiker with the group.

Too large a group is unwieldy and diminishes the wilderness experience for yourself and others. The park limits group size to a maximum of fifteen people, but an ideal size is probably four. In case of injury, one can stay with the victim, while the other two can hike out for help. Thus no one is left alone. In addition, most of the backcountry campsites in the Chisos Mountains will not accommodate more than six people.

Leave your travel plans with friends so that they can send help if you do not appear. Allow plenty of time before help is sent; trips often run later than expected.

Ideally, you should never hike alone, especially cross-country or on the park's lightly traveled trails. That said, if you do hike alone, inform family or friends of your specific travel plans. Because of the large number of hikers at Big Bend, the park staff cannot keep track of the whereabouts of every hiker. Once you set up your hiking itinerary, do not deviate from it. Otherwise, rescuers will be unable to find you.

A hiker looks across the desert from the Southeast ▶
Rim of the Chisos Mountains.

Upon returning from your hike, immediately call to let your friends know of your return. Never forget to check in at the end of your hike. Nothing will aggravate rescuers more than to find that you were at a bar in Terlingua relaxing with a beer while they were stumbling around in the rain and dark looking for you.

On short busy hikes or nature trails, such as those at Santa Elena Canyon or Hot Springs, where plenty of other people are around should a mishap occur, such precautions may not be necessary.

Water

Because of the heat and dry air at Big Bend, you must drink plenty of water. In summer, at least a gallon per day is necessary on long hikes. Since many of the springs at Big Bend are unreliable and dependent on recent rainfall, plan to carry all the water you will need. On some of the longer desert hikes it can be physically difficult to carry enough. Springs can help supplement the supply, but be sure to check ahead of time to learn the springs' current status. Regardless of their believed status, try not to arrive at a spring without at least some water. If the spring had just gone dry, you could be in a difficult situation without some reserve water.

Because water sources may be contaminated, any water used should be purified before use. You may not get sick if unpurified water is obtained directly from the head of a spring in a little-used area. However, it is best to play it safe and always treat your water.

Boiling vigorously for ten minutes is a reliable method, but slow and fuel consuming. Mechanical filtration units are available at most outdoors shops. Filters with very small pores strain out bacteria, viruses, cysts, and other microorganisms. Their ability to filter out the smallest organisms, such as viruses, varies from model to model. For very contaminated water, filtration should probably be used in conjunction with chemical treatment.

Chemical treatment is probably the easiest method, but may not be as effective as filtering. Chlorination is the method used by many municipal water systems, but the use of hyperiodide tablets is probably more controllable and reliable for backpackers. They can be purchased at any outdoors store. Follow the directions carefully. Cold or cloudy water requires more chemical use or longer treatment times. The cleaner that your water is from the start, the better.

Get your water from springs or upstream from trails and camps if possible. Water taken from tinajas and particularly the Rio Grande is of dubious quality. Except in an emergency, it is best to avoid Rio Grande water altogether. For day hikes, it is usually easier just to carry sufficient water for the day.

The park allows hikers doing long hikes to cache water along the route ahead of time. If you do cache water for a hike, write your name and expected removal date on the container. Do not leave water caches in historic buildings or other popular visitor use areas. Leave food only if it is stored in a commercial bear-proof canister.

Stream Crossings

Crossing all but the smallest of streams poses several hazards. In the desert country at Big Bend, streams are rare and small and generally pose little difficulty in crossing. Except during a flash flood, few of the drainages along the trails in this guide carry any water at all. If any do flood, however, do not attempt to cross them. Just wait; such floods subside very quickly, usually within a few hours at most. When crossing one of the few creeks that often carry water, such as Terlingua or Tornillo Creeks, try to find a broad, slow-moving stretch for your ford. Be careful hopping from rock to rock; they are often unstable and slippery, and can cause a fall or twisted ankle. Undo the waist strap on your backpack for quick removal if necessary. If the water is deep or swift-moving, use a stout walking stick for stability, or even a rope.

The Rio Grande is the one significant waterway in the park. Because of its strong currents, deep holes, invisible bottom, and poor water quality, do not swim in or try to cross the river.

Insects

One of the pleasures of hiking at Big Bend is its paucity of nuisance insects. However, mosquitoes will hatch after heavy rains, even in desert regions of the park. The most likely time is late summer. A repellent containing DEET will discourage mosquitoes and gnats from bothering you. Camp well away from the river, water holes, streams, and other wet areas. Good mosquito netting on your tent will allow a pleasant night's sleep. Usually mosquitoes are no problem at all.

A tent will also keep out nocturnal creatures such as scorpions and centipedes. Bites and stings from scorpions and centipedes found at Big Bend are painful but not usually serious. As long as you use a tent and refrain from turning over rocks or logs, you are unlikely to see any.

Ticks are rare at Big Bend, unlike in much of Central and East Texas. However, they can carry serious diseases, such as Rocky Mountain spotted fever and Lyme disease, so be aware of them. Use insect repellent and check yourself every night, especially if you have been moving through brush or tall grass. If a tick attaches, remove it promptly. Use tweezers and avoid squeezing the tick as you pull it out. Do not leave the head embedded and do not handle the tick. Apply antiseptic to the bite and wash thoroughly. If you develop a rash or any illness within two or three weeks of the bite, see a doctor.

Bears and Mountain Lions

Grizzlies have not roamed Texas for decades, so bear attacks are extremely unlikely. Except for a few black bears found in the Guadalupe Mountains, bears have been virtually extinct in Texas since the 1930s. In recent years, however, a small number of black bears have begun to recolonize the Chisos Mountains. The bears migrated north from the Sierra del Carmen in Mexico, possibly because increased protection in Mexico has led to population growth. These migrants have reproduced and established a small population. The bears are scarce, so you are unlikely to encounter them. If you do, consider yourself lucky. Very few Texans have ever seen a bear in the wild. Give any that you see a wide berth, especially those with cubs. If one approaches, yell, make loud noises, wave your arms, and throw rocks. Remain standing to appear large and don't run away. Check with a ranger for new information before you hike. These recommendations apply only to the bears at Big Bend; other parks and places may have a different situation and advice.

When backpacking, a few precautions will prevent any bear problems. Put all food and other smelly items, such as soap, toothpaste, deodorant, perfume, utensils, water bottles, pots and pans, stoves, and garbage, into the bear-proof boxes found at the primitive campsites in the Chisos Mountains. Leave your packs unzipped to prevent damage to them by a nosy animal. Never cook in your tent or keep food in your tent or sleeping bag. If a bear does somehow take your food, don't even think about trying to get it back. If bears eat human food and become habituated to it, they could be a threat to future visitors and might have to be killed, so do your best to prevent them from obtaining food. Encounters with bears are unlikely in the desert areas of the park.

The mountain lions in the Chisos Mountains have lost some of their fear of humans after years with no hunting. On rare occasions, hikers have encountered them on the trail. There have been three non-fatal attacks since 1984, not many when you consider how many people hike in the park every year. If you do see a lion, you are among a fortunate few; they are very reclusive. If the lion does not immediately run away, stand your ground, ideally near others to appear large. Do not crouch or play dead. Shout, wave your arms, and throw rocks. Don't act like prey by running away or screaming. Other actions to avoid include hiking alone or at night. Keep small children close to you. Check with park rangers for more advice on handling such an encounter.

Snakes

The vast majority of snakes that you will encounter (usually you will see none) are nonpoisonous. On rare occasions you may encounter a rattlesnake or, even more rarely, a copperhead. Most are not aggressive and will not strike unless stepped on or otherwise provoked. In daytime or cold weather they are usually holed up under rocks and in cracks. The most likely time to see them is during warm evenings when they come out to hunt. If you watch your step, don't hike at dusk or at night, and don't put your hands or feet under rocks, ledges, and other places that you cannot see, you should never have any problem. Don't hurt or kill any that you find. Remember, snakes are important predators.

If bitten by a poisonous snake, get medical help as soon as possible. Treatment methods are controversial and beyond the scope of this book. Fortunately, the majority of bites do not inject a significant amount of venom. Bites by nonpoisonous snakes should be kept clean to prevent infection.

Equipment

The most important outdoor equipment is probably your footwear. Hiking boots should be sturdy and comfortable. Lightweight leather and nylon boots are probably adequate for all but rugged trails and for carrying heavy packs. Proper clothing, plenty of food and water, and a pack are other necessities. Other vital items for every trip include waterproof matches, rain gear or some sort of emergency shelter, a pocketknife, a signal mirror and whistle, a first-aid kit, a detailed map, and a compass.

Because Big Bend tends to be warm, shorts are popular for hiking. On well-used and maintained trails, shorts do fine. However, on lightly used trails and cross-country routes, be sure to wear long pants. Many plants at Big Bend have thorns and spines to protect themselves from foraging animals. These plants can wreak havoc on uncovered skin. If you do wear shorts, be sure to use sunscreen. Sunscreen and a broad-brimmed hat are vital to protect other parts of the body as well from the strong sun at Big Bend.

In general, all of your outdoor equipment should be as light and small as possible. Many excellent books and outdoors shops will help you select the proper boots, tents, sleeping bags, cooking utensils, and other equipment necessary for your hikes.

Getting Lost

Careful use of maps and hike descriptions should prevent you from ever getting lost. However, if you should become lost or disoriented, immediately stop. Charging around blindly will only worsen the problem. Careful study of the map, compass, and surrounding landmarks in Big Bend's open country will often reorient you. If you can retrace your route, follow it until you are oriented again. Do not proceed unless you are sure of your location. If you left travel plans with friends or family, rescuers should find you soon.

Often a standard response if lost is to follow a drainage downstream. In most areas of the country, it will eventually lead you to a trail, road, or town. However, at Big Bend, it may well take you deeper into the backcountry instead and cannot be recommended. In addition, that strategy will probably take you farther away from rescuers.

Most of the trails in this guide are well-maintained and marked and easy to follow. However, a significant number, such as the Strawhouse, Mesa de Anguila, and Devil's Den hikes, are very lightly used and maintained little if at all. These types of routes should only be done by experienced hikers well equipped with topographic maps and a compass. Piles of rocks called cairns often mark the less-traveled routes. A few routes have no markers or defined path at all. Read each hike description carefully to determine any difficulties in route-finding before you start.

On some hikes, exposed bedrock worn or scratched by the hooves of horses or past mule trains will sometimes help you stay on the route. Trails often follow the easiest terrain. If you have lost the trail, look carefully on the most gentle slopes, the lowest passes, and the flattest benches for signs of the trail. Switchbacks usually indicate a trail; animals do not create them.

If you are lost, the use of signals may help rescuers find you. A series of three flashes or noises is the universal distress signal. Use the whistle or signal mirror. Provided that it can be done safely, making a small, smoky fire may help rescuers find you.

Vehicle Safety

Use care when driving the park's roads to the trailheads. More serious accidents probably occur on park roads than on the trails. Obey the park speed limit and any warning signs. At night, watch carefully for wildlife on the road.

Most of this guide's hikes have trailheads that can be reached by any car. Some, as noted, require high clearance and a few may require four-wheel drive, especially in wet weather. Rain or snow can temporarily make even a good road impassable. Before venturing onto Big Bend's dirt roads, you should check with a park ranger at any visitor center. On the less-traveled back roads, you should carry basic emergency equipment, such as a shovel, chains, water, a spare tire, a jack, blankets, and some extra food and clothing. Make sure that your vehicle is in good operating condition with a full tank of gas.

Theft and vandalism occasionally occur at trailheads, particularly along the river. Park rangers can tell you of any recent problems. Try not to leave valuables in the car at all; if you must, lock them out of sight in the trunk. Ideally, put everything out of sight to give the vehicle an overall empty appearance.

How to Use This Book

This guide is comprehensive and contains most of the major trails and routes found in Big Bend National Park. The park offers a wide range of hiking experiences, from easy 0.25-mile paved routes to rugged cross-country backpacks. The majority of trailheads in this book are accessible by any type of vehicle; only a few require high- clearance or four-wheel-drive vehicles. Each description elaborates on any special road conditions.

If you are a beginning hiker, don't let the length of some of these trails intimidate you. You don't need to restrict yourself to only the short ones. Most of the long hikes are very beautiful and rewarding even if you only go 0.5 mile down the trail.

Although just the trails in this guide may keep you busy for years, many of the hike descriptions suggest additional nearby routes. As you gain experience, don't be afraid to try them.

This book describes trails, routes, and trail complexes scattered widely across Big Bend National Park. The park map at the start of this book indicates their locations. Several categories of information describe each hike. The general description category gives a brief, one-sentence description of the hike. The hiking speed of different people varies considerably, though we are estimating approximate hiking time at 2 miles an hour. A hike is loosely classed as a day hike if most reasonably fit people can easily complete it round-trip in one day or less. Hikes long or difficult enough to be classed as backpacks usually require one or more nights on the trail.

Except for loop trails, the distance given is usually the one-way mileage. There is sometimes some disagreement about distance between maps, published sources, and trail signs. The distance given in this guide is the authors' best estimate using these sources. Many trails require a return on the same route, so the total mileage will usually be double that shown. Some of the trails, such as the Chimneys and Dodson Trails, can be done one-way if a car shuttle is set up ahead of time.

The difficulty rating gives a general idea of the physical effort necessary to complete the trail. This rating takes into account the trail's length and condition. Problems in route-finding add to the trail's difficulty. In general, easy trails can by done without difficulty by any person in reasonable physical condition. Moderate trails usually require significant physical effort, but are not difficult for hikers in good physical condition. Strenuous trails require considerable effort and should only be done by people in very good condition. Many of the strenuous trails in this guide are well-maintained and easy to follow, but some require extensive route-finding and map-reading ability. A few of the easier routes also require some route-finding ability, so be sure to read the trail description ahead of time.

The traffic category is meant to give at least a rough idea of trail usage. Without elaborate hiker counting done over an extended period of time, it is difficult to come up with a purely objective measure of usage. However, on a trail designated as receiving very light use, it is rare to see other hikers. On those designated as having light use, meetings with other hikers are uncommon. On trails marked moderate, you will see at least a few other hikers on most trips. On those marked heavy, you will generally meet several other hiking parties. Realize that trail use is somewhat seasonal. Trail usage overall is lighter at Big Bend during the summer, especially on the desert hikes. During Thanksgiving, Christmas vacation, and college spring break, trail usage increases on all routes.

This book uses elevation profiles to provide an idea of the length and elevation of hills you will encounter along each hike. In the profiles the vertical axes of the graphs show the distance climbed in feet. In contrast, the horizontal axes show the distance traveled in miles. It is important to understand that the vertical (feet) and horizontal (miles) scales can differ between hikes. Read each profile carefully making sure you read both the height and distance shown. This will help you interpret what you see in each profile. Some elevation profiles may show gradual hills to be steep or steep hills to be gradual. Elevation profiles may not be provided for hikes with little or no elevation gain.

The topo maps category gives the names of the United States Geological Survey 7.5-minute topographic maps necessary for the trail. These maps are available at the Panther Junction Visitor Center and many outdoors shops in Texas. The Trails Illustrated Big Bend National Park map, also available at the visitor center and outdoors shops, is generally adequate for most of the trails with moderate or heavy traffic. However, it is critical to have the topographic maps and a compass on the less-traveled trails and routes. Read each description carefully and talk to park rangers ahead of time to help determine the need for topographic maps. A few errors, particularly trail routing errors, exist in both the Trails Illustrated map and the topographic maps. Those errors of which the authors are aware are mentioned in the trail descriptions.

The finding the trailhead entry provides detailed directions for locating the start of each hike. With a basic park map, you can easily locate the trailhead from the directions. Distances were measured using a car odometer or mile markers. Realize that different cars will vary slightly in their measurements. Be sure to keep an eye open for the specific signs, junctions, and landmarks mentioned in the directions, not just the mileage.

The hike entry provides a detailed description of the trail itself, often accompanied by historical, biological, and geological information about the area through which the trail passes. Following this is miles and directions, a mile-by-mile summary of junctions and major landmarks along the trail. These mileages were generally estimated from the topographic maps and may be a bit conservative.

Detailed maps accompany each trail description. The map information was taken from USGS topographic maps and national park maps. Use the guidebook's maps in conjunction with the topographic maps and the Trails Illustrated map.

The maps in this book that depict a detailed close-up of an area use elevation tints, called hypsometry, to portray relief. Each gray tone represents a range of equal elevation, as shown in the scale key with the map. These maps will give you a good idea of elevation gain and loss. The darker tones are lower elevations and the lighter grays are higher elevations. The lighter the tone, the higher the elevation. Narrow bands of different gray tones spaced closely together indicate steep terrain, whereas wider bands indicate areas of more gradual slope.

After reading the trail descriptions and assessing your desires and abilities, pick a hike that appeals. Then pack your gear and hit the trail!

Park Information

Superintendent
Big Bend National Park, Texas 79834
(432) 477–2251

Map Legend

— - —   Park Boundary

395   U.S. Highway

118   State Highway

170   Forest Road

——————   Other Paved Road

═══════   Gravel Road

====   Unimproved Road

------   Trail

—·—·—   Shared Trail

=====   Highlighted Route

Lake/Large River

River/Creek

⌀̃   Spring

⫽   Waterfall/Pour-off

≍   Bridge

Δ   Campground

†   Cemetery/Grave

▲   Mountain/Peak

9   Hike Number from this book

27   Hike Direction

◻   Overlook/Viewpoint

)(Pass

■   Point of Interest

▮   Ranger Station

🚶   Trailhead

+   UTM Grid Tick

Big Bend
National Park

1 South Rim via Pinnacles and Boot Canyon Trails (and Emory Peak)

General description: A backpack or long day hike to the South Rim of the Chisos Mountains via the Pinnacles and Boot Canyon Trails.
Distance: 6.3 miles one way.
Approximate hiking time: 3 to 3.5 hours.

Difficulty: Strenuous.
Traffic: Heavy.
Trail surface: Dirt path.
Topo maps: The Basin and Emory Peak.

Finding the trailhead: The trail starts in the Basin at the main trailhead located near the Basin store, visitor center, and lodge.

From the store, follow the sidewalk downhill to the west to the main trailhead sign.

The Hike

The Pinnacles Trail climbs into the Chisos Mountains to the South Rim, a sheer escarpment on the south side of the high section of the mountains. Views encompass thousands of square miles of desert and mountains, making this one of the most impressive hikes in the park.

From the Basin, the Pinnacles Trail climbs steeply through oaks, pines, junipers, and madrone trees to a high saddle between Toll Mountain and Emory Peak. At this pass, the trail levels out. From here, spectacular views of the Basin, the Window, and the desert far to the west attract the eye.

The junction with the Emory Peak Trail lies about 0.1 mile down the trail from the saddle; bear left unless you wish to climb Emory Peak. The right-hand trail, a 1-mile spur, leads to the summit of Emory Peak, the highest point in the Chisos Mountains. It climbs steeply and requires a bit of rock scrambling at the end. Sheer, vertigo-inducing cliffs drop off from the summit on several sides. Views from the summit cover 360 degrees and encompass almost the entire park and far beyond.

If you climb Emory Peak, return by the same spur trail to continue toward the South Rim on the main trail. The trail mileages listed do not include the spur trail to Emory Peak. The Pinnacles Trail is often called the Boot Canyon or Boot Spring Trail after the junction with the Emory Peak Trail. It winds through Boot Canyon, so named because of a large, prominent rock formation shaped like an upside-down cowboy boot. The only spring in the high Chisos Mountains that produces enough water to be useful to humans lies in Boot Canyon, but it flows only intermittently. Do not rely on obtaining water from Boot Spring; carry what you need from the trailhead.

Boot Canyon in the Chisos Mountains is surprisingly lush. ▶

South Rim via Pinnacles and Boot Canyon Trails (and Emory Peak); South Rim via Laguna Meadow Trail (and Colima Trail); Southeast and Northeast Rim

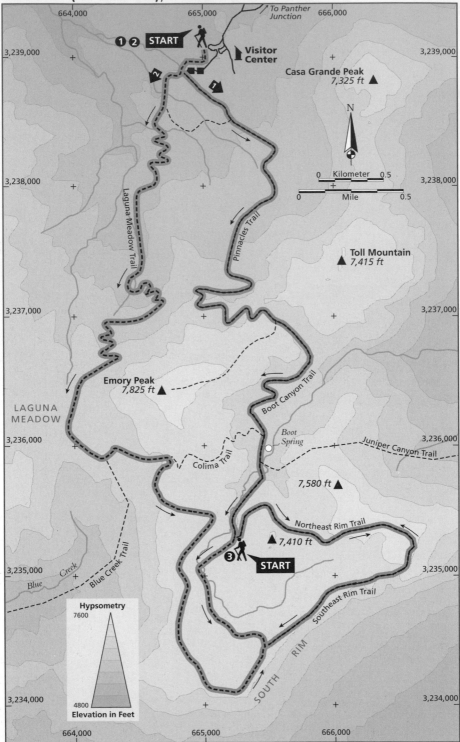

From Emory Peak, the view encompasses 360 degrees of mountains and desert.

Bigtooth maple trees shade portions of the Boot Canyon Trail as it winds past seasonal pools of water. The route passes several trail junctions in Boot Canyon, as listed with the trail mileages. Follow the signs and stay with the Boot Canyon Trail all the way to the South Rim.

The South Rim is one of the most scenic areas of the park; vast stretches of Chihuahuan Desert sweep south from the mountain foothills 2,500 vertical feet below. The Rio Grande, almost a vertical mile below and far to the south, and mountains in Mexico are visible on a clear day. Because of this tremendous panorama, the South Rim draws many hikers and backpackers. From the South Rim, trails lead to the Northeast Rim and back to the Basin via Laguna Meadow.

In late summer and early fall, evergreen and littleleaf sumac bear tart, edible berries, and pinyon pines produce edible nuts that ripen later in the fall. Claret-cup cactus and prickly pear can be found blooming along these trails from April through June, and summer and fall are the best times to see wildflowers along the Pinnacles and Boot Canyon Trails.

Mountain sage, scarlet bouvardia, two species of penstemon, and skyrocket gilia all have bright red, tubular flowers. Heliopsis has a common yellow sunflower-type

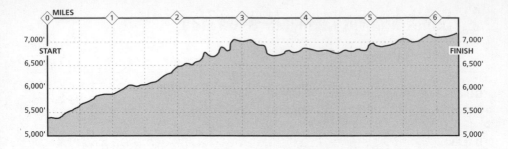

bloom. The delicate blue plains flax and dark blue dayflowers can be found along shadier sections of the trail.

Look in shady places under pine trees for Mexican squawroot, with its unusual pale yellow stalk that resembles a corn cob with yellow flowers in place of kernels. The parasitic squawroot obtains nutrition from pine, oak, and madrone roots below the soil surface and lacks the chlorophyll that makes most plants look green.

The same summer thundershowers that bring wildflowers produce lightning and strong winds; watch the weather as you hike and avoid the South Rim, Emory Peak, and other exposed areas during storms. Be sure to carry plenty of warm, dry clothing, even in summer; thunderstorms can make it quite cool and wet. Although winters are generally mild, occasional storms bring snow and cold temperatures to the high mountains traversed by this trail.

Miles and Directions

0.0 Trailhead. At the initial junction, follow the left fork south, toward the South Rim. It drops slightly and leaves the developed area.

0.5 Trail junction. Follow the Pinnacles Trail to the left.

3.4 The trail levels out on the saddle between Toll Mountain and Emory Peak.

3.5 Junction with Emory Peak Trail. Stay left.

4.5 Junction with Colima Trail. Go straight on the Boot Canyon Trail.

4.8 Junction with Juniper Canyon Trail. Go straight on the Boot Canyon Trail.

5.3 Junction with Northeast Rim Trail. Go right on the Boot Canyon Trail.

6.3 The South Rim.

2 South Rim via Laguna Meadow Trail (and Colima Trail)

General description: A backpack or long day hike to the South Rim of the Chisos Mountains.

Distance: 6.3 miles one way.

Approximate hiking time: 3 to 3.5 hours.

Difficulty: Strenuous.

Traffic: Heavy.

Trail surface: Dirt path.

Topo maps: The Basin and Emory Peak.

Finding the trailhead: The trail starts in the Basin at the main trailhead located near the Basin store, visitor center, and lodge.

From the store, follow the sidewalk downhill to the west to the MAIN TRAILHEAD sign.

The Hike

The South Rim is probably the classic hike of Texas. Although the trip is fairly strenuous, almost any Texas hiker worth his or her salt will someday try to hike to the South Rim. Few other hikes in Texas can surpass the quality and sheer quantity of views along the trail. On clear days, the views cover most of the Texas Big Bend country and far into Mexico.

To fully enjoy the trip, try to allow two or three days on the trail. People in good shape can do the round-trip hike in one day, however. Not surprisingly, the hike is popular. Although there are many designated primitive campsites, it may be difficult to obtain one during Thanksgiving or college spring break.

This route to the South Rim is less steep than the other primary route using the Pinnacles and Boot Canyon Trails, although it still requires the same net elevation gain. Often the two routes are combined into a loop trip. Water can sometimes be obtained in a pinch at Boot Spring, but do not count on it without checking on the spring's status before you start; it does dry up at times. It is best to carry all the water you will need.

The hike will be hot in summer, but the terrain is high and wooded enough for the trek to be enjoyable. Get an early start for the climb out of the Basin. The trail is also good in winter, but be prepared for the occasional winter storm. The mountains usually get a few snows every year, but these are usually light and short-lived.

The trail starts from the bottom of the parking lot and immediately hits a three-way junction. As with all trail junctions in the Chisos Mountains, this one is well marked. Go left, toward the South Rim. The trail forks again in a short distance; go right onto the Laguna Meadow Trail. Ignore the Chisos Basin Loop Trail forking left after about 0.5 mile.

The trail climbs steadily south up a drainage below Emory Peak. Multiple switchbacks take you higher and higher until the trail reaches a small divide at the

On a clear day, the view from the South Rim stretches far into Mexico.

head of the drainage. To most hikers' relief, the trail ceases climbing for a short distance as it crosses the grassy flats of Laguna Meadow. Junipers and pinyons dot the small valley. A fire swept through here a number of years ago, burning some of the forest, but there are still good shade trees under which you can relax before resuming the climb.

From Laguna Meadow, the trail climbs southeast below the rocky talus slopes of Emory Peak. Look carefully at the talus slopes; a few aspens cling to life, remnants of a cooler, wetter climate that once allowed aspens, Douglas-firs, Arizona pines, and other trees to thrive in the Chisos Mountains. Today, only a few scattered stands of these trees still live.

The Blue Creek Trail forks to the right only a short distance above Laguna Meadow. Continue climbing toward the South Rim. After less than a mile, the Colima Trail turns off to the left. It is a shortcut to Boot Canyon and Boot Spring. Continue straight toward the South Rim. The trail soon levels out, and the rest of the hike to the South Rim is relatively easy.

The South Rim is a large escarpment along the southern edge of the high part of the Chisos Mountains. From the rim, the mountains drop off in precipitous cliffs

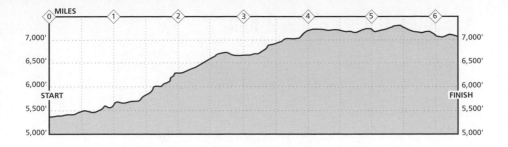

and steep, rubble-choked slopes to the desert thousands of feet below. Views stretch for miles, far beyond the Rio Grande into Mexico. If you are camping, there are few better places in Texas to watch the sunrise and sunset. Unfortunately, in recent years the views have greatly declined in quality as Mexico has developed new power plants and industries with few pollution controls. When added to pollution from American sources, the haze greatly diminishes the view.

The trail follows the rim to the northeast, going a short distance to the junction with the Boot Canyon and Southeast Rim Trails. Both are very scenic trails that offer good potential as loop routes when combined with this trail.

Miles and Directions

0.0 Basin trailhead.

3.8 Junction with Blue Creek Trail just past Laguna Meadow. Stay left.

4.6 Junction with the Colima Trail. Go straight toward the South Rim.

6.3 Junction with Boot Canyon and Southeast Rim Trails on South Rim.

3 Southeast and Northeast Rim

General description: A day hike along a very scenic section of the South Rim of the Chisos Mountains.

Distance: 3.3 miles one way.

Approximate hiking time: 1.5 to 2 hours.

Difficulty: Easy to moderate.

Traffic: Moderate.

Trail surface: Dirt path.

Topo map: Emory Peak.

Finding the trailhead: This trail forms a side loop off the Boot Canyon Trail. The trail can be hiked in either direction. In this description, the trail is described traveling from the north end in Boot Canyon to the south end on the South Rim.

The Hike

This trail makes a loop along the Northeast, East, and Southeast Rim sections of the South Rim area of the high Chisos Mountains. A high, sheer escarpment characterizes the South Rim, where the scrub woodland of the Chisos drops rapidly down into the Chihuahuan Desert below. The high elevation and steep cliffs along this route offer some of the best views in Texas.

This hike is usually done as part of a combination with the Laguna Meadow, Boot Canyon, or Pinnacles Trails. Although the combined trails can be done as a long, strenuous day hike, most people do the hike as a one- or two-night backpack. Water can sometimes be obtained at Boot Spring, but it is not a reliable source. Plan to carry all that you need.

Peregrine falcons often nest along the section of the South Rim traversed by this trail. If falcons are in residence, this trail is generally closed from early spring to midsummer. Be sure to ask about the trail's status before hiking all the way up to it.

The upper parts of the Chisos Mountains harbor a small area of woodland surrounded by a sea of desert. The high elevations are cooler and attract additional precipitation that allows trees to grow. Most of the woodland consists of a scrubby forest of pinyon pine, juniper, and oak. One tree, the Mexican drooping juniper, noticeable because it looks perpetually wilted, is found in no other site in the United States. Another tree, the Chisos oak, is not known to occur anywhere else.

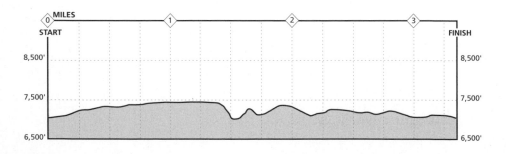

Rugged foothills of the Chisos Mountains lie far below the cliffs of the Southeast Rim.

In more sheltered areas of the mountains, such as Boot Canyon where this trail starts, protection from wind and sun allow scattered stands of Arizona pine, Arizona cypress, bigtooth maple, and Douglas-fir to grow. These trees were more common in times past when the climate was cooler and wetter.

The trail starts in the bottom of Boot Canyon at a fork with the Boot Canyon Trail. It climbs steadily out of the canyon, heading east overall. After a mile or so, the trail reaches the high point of the hike and levels out as it nears the Northeast Rim. Views stretching northeast across Juniper Canyon to Crown Mountain and beyond are tremendous. The trail gradually turns south and then southwest as it curves around the various sections of the South Rim, following the edge of the massive escarpment for much of the way. New views continually open up of vast sweeps of mountain and desert. If the light is right, silver glints of sun reveal the Rio Grande far to the south.

Unfortunately, new power plants and industrial developments in Mexico have been built without strong pollution controls. When combined with pollution from American sources, the resulting haze sometimes mars the views from the Chisos

Mountains. In addition, acid rain and other environmental problems may be resulting from the pollution.

The trail ends at a junction with the Boot Canyon Trail at its terminus on the South Rim. If time allows, plan to spend a night or two somewhere on or near the South Rim. It is hard to find a better spot to watch the sunrise or sunset in Texas.

Miles and Directions

0.0 Trailhead at junction with Boot Canyon Trail.

1.4 Northeast Rim.

3.3 Junction with Boot Canyon Trail on South Rim.

4 Juniper Canyon

General description: A day hike or backpack down one of the major canyons that drains the high Chisos Mountains.

Distance: 6.2 miles one way.

Approximate hiking time: 3 to 3.5 hours.

Difficulty: Strenuous.

Traffic: Light.

Trail surface: Dirt path.

Topo maps: The Basin, Emory Peak, and Glenn Spring.

Finding the trailhead: The trail is reached on foot by taking the Pinnacles and Boot Spring Trails to Boot Canyon. The Pinnacles Trail starts at the Chisos Basin trailhead by the Basin store and visitor center. It is 4.8 miles from the Basin trailhead to the start of the Juniper Canyon Trail in Boot Canyon.

The lower trailhead of the Juniper Canyon Trail lies at the end of the dirt Juniper Canyon Road. The road is a spur off of Glenn Spring Road. Both roads usually require high clearance or four-wheel drive; check with a ranger for current road conditions.

The Hike

Hikers often take the Juniper Canyon Trail as part of the Outer Mountain Loop, but it is worthy of a long day hike as well if hiked from the lower trailhead at the end of Juniper Canyon Road. When hiked as part of the Outer Mountain Loop, backpackers combine it with the Dodson and Blue Creek Trails. When the Juniper Canyon Trail is combined with other trails, it usually requires a multi-day backpack. If a shuttle is arranged, the trail can be done as a strenuous one-way day hike between the Basin and the Juniper Canyon Road trailheads.

The upper part of the Juniper Canyon Trail is generally warm but pleasant in summer. The lower parts can get quite hot, however. Although winters are usually temperate, fall and spring are probably the ideal times for the hike.

The trail begins in the Chisos Mountains in Boot Canyon, climbs a short distance, then descends fairly steeply through pinyon pine, oak, and juniper to Upper

Juniper Canyon

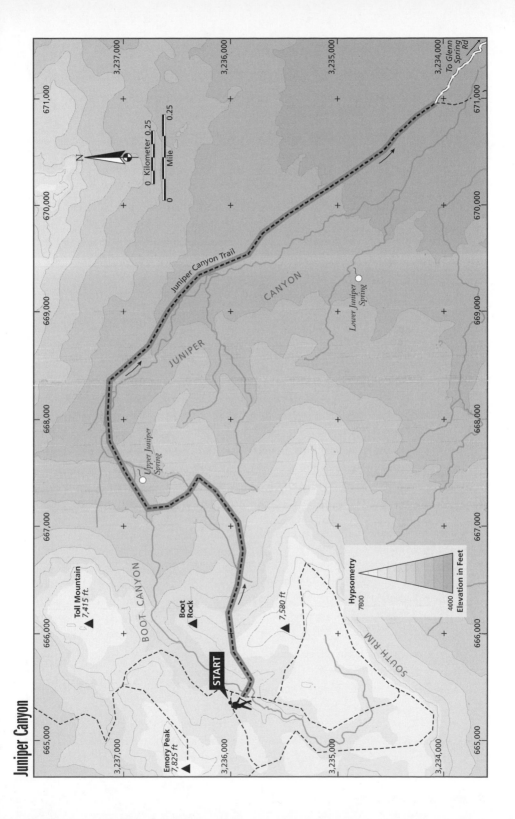

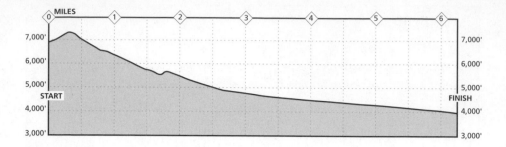

Juniper Spring. The section of trail from Boot Canyon to the spring is closed to camping except in designated sites; campers should look for sites below the short spur trail to the spring. The route up and down Juniper Canyon is used by many animals in addition to hikers, so campers should take precautions to avoid encounters with black bears.

Upper Juniper Spring, set in a lovely grove of oaks, does not flow reliably year-round, so be sure to carry plenty of water. If you do collect water here, purify it before drinking. Several rectangular concrete stock tanks, pipes, and lengths of fence wire remain from Big Bend's ranching era. Early landowners went to great lengths to provide water for their stock by clearing out springs, building tanks such as these, and sometimes even pumping water up steep slopes to pastures. In the early 1900s, ranchers considered grasslands in the canyons and higher elevations of the Chisos Mountains to be some of the best grazing lands in West Texas.

Below Upper Juniper Spring, the terrain gradually becomes less steep and the trail enters more grasslands, punctuated by sotol and the occasional juniper tree. Pleasant campsites can be found in this area. Hikers traveling the trail in spring may notice a heavy grape-like fragrance; look for the purple flower clusters and shiny deep green leaves of Texas mountain laurel lining the trail and washes. At the end of Juniper Canyon Road, the trail ends and the east end of the Dodson Trail starts.

Miles and Directions

0.0   Start of Juniper Canyon Trail in Boot Canyon.

2.6   Upper Juniper Spring.

6.2   Lower trailhead at Juniper Canyon Road.

5 Dodson

General description: A backpack, extended backpack, or long day hike between Juniper Canyon and Homer Wilson Blue Creek Ranch.
Distance: 9.9 miles one way.
Approximate hiking time: 5 hours.

Difficulty: Strenuous.
Traffic: Light.
Trail surface: Dirt path.
Topo maps: Emory Peak and Glenn Spring.

Finding the trailhead: The Dodson Trail has two trailheads, one at each end. The eastern trailhead is located at the end of Juniper Canyon Road, a primitive dirt road that joins Glenn Spring Road 1.5 miles north of Glenn Spring. This is also a trailhead of the Juniper Canyon Trail, forming a connection between the two trails.

The western trailhead is at Homer Wilson Blue Creek Ranch, located along the Ross Maxwell Scenic Drive 8.1 miles south of its junction with the Panther Junction-Study Butte highway. One trailhead of the Blue Creek Trail also lies here, so hikers may continue directly from the Dodson Trail onto the Blue Creek Trail. Homer Wilson Blue Creek Ranch is a convenient site for backpackers traveling the Outer Mountain Loop to cache water ahead of time. Do not leave water caches in the historic ranch buildings; hide them in the desert. Write your name and expected removal date on the containers. Leave food only if it is stored in a commercial bear-proof canister.

The Hike

The Dodson Trail crosses the rugged, mountainous terrain of the northern Sierra Quemada (Spanish for "burned mountains"), a southern extension of the Chisos Mountains. Passing below the South Rim of the high Chisos, the trail crosses several major drainages, including Juniper Draw, Fresno Creek, Smoky Creek, and Blue Creek. Hikers must therefore cross the high ridges that divide these drainages, repeatedly gaining then losing elevation. The total elevation gain is thus more than just the difference between the highest and lowest points of the hike. The trail requires a total gain of about 2,000 feet traveling east to west and 1,800 feet traveling west to east. However, at the high points, broad wilderness vistas reward hikers for their exertions.

Part or all of the Dodson Trail may be hiked in conjunction with other trails, including Juniper Canyon Trail, Elephant Tusk Trail, Smoky Creek Trail, and Blue Creek Trail. Probably the most common combination is the Outer Mountain Loop, which combines the Juniper Canyon and Blue Creek Trails with this hike.

The Dodson Trail passes through a broad ecotone between the forested Chisos Mountains and the arid desert. Ecotones are borders or transition zones between ecologic zones. Here it shares characteristics of both mountain and desert, so you may find moisture-loving plants such as oak, fern, and mountain laurel growing in isolated pockets in sheltered canyons as well as dry desert plants growing on exposed slopes and ridges.

The Dodson Trail winds through the hills between Elephant Tusk, shown here, and this photo's viewpoint on the South Rim.

Plants and animals that live in an ecotone may be outside of their ideal environment. When they try to live in this marginal habitat, individuals are often forced to adapt to new conditions. When successful, they may pass on these new traits to their offspring, providing a versatility that may help the species cope with changes in the climate. Given isolation and enough time, a new subspecies or even a new species may arise.

Some plants are adapted to handle the large climatic fluctuations that occur in ecotones and are able to take advantage of the distinctive environment. Cacti have a unique structure that permits their cells to swell dramatically without bursting. This allows them to store large amounts of intracellular water during the infrequent rains so that they can survive long dry spells. Ocotillos have a dual-strategy root system, with spreading near-surface roots that collect moisture during light rains, as well as a tap root to exploit deeper water sources.

Remains of corrals, dams, and ruined ranch houses in the foothills along the Dodson Trail provide mute evidence of frontier ranching during the first half of the twentieth century. The rich, arid grasslands that attracted ranchers to the Big Bend were destroyed by overgrazing within fifty years. Without grasses to protect the fertile soil and slow water runoff, erosion stripped the soil away. With the land's lessened ability to retain moisture, springs and creeks sometimes dried up.

Grasses along the Dodson Trail are recovering from overgrazing that occurred before the park was created. Juniper trees may also be making a limited comeback after being heavily cut for fence posts. However, grasslands still have not recovered in the lower elevations of the park despite sixty years of protection. The destruction happened quickly; recovery is slow.

Hikers should not attempt the Dodson Trail without the 7.5-minute USGS topographic maps, a compass, and the ability to read them. Plenty of water and good judgment are additional requirements. Be aware that parts of the trail follow a route significantly different than that shown on the maps. Some sections of the trail follow dry washes. Because flash floods can quickly wipe out any trail markers in these drainages, hikers must watch carefully to find the points where the trail exits the wash.

Although numerous springs are marked on the maps, most are ephemeral and cannot be relied upon. Fresno Creek is most likely to have water, but it too can be dry. Rangers may be able to advise you on water availability; however, wise hikers always carry plenty of liquid. Many animals, including humans, depend on springs; please take care not to contaminate any water source. Always purify water taken from them.

The trail description is based upon an east-to-west hike from the Juniper Canyon trailhead to Homer Wilson Blue Creek Ranch. Starting from the trailhead at the end of Juniper Canyon Road, follow the trail south across open desert to reach the main drainage of Juniper Draw. The trail then proceeds west up the drainage, passing in and out of the wash, and reaches the ruins of Dodson Ranch near Dodson Spring. Campsites must be located at least 100 yards from any historic structure or spring; collecting or damaging any artifact or structure is strictly prohibited.

This part of the trail follows the route used by Harve Dodson to reach his ranch headquarters, which was more than 3.5 miles from the nearest wagon road. The only access was by horse or on foot, and all supplies had to be packed in on horseback to the ranch house. When an early visitor asked how he moved his family into such a remote and rugged place, Dodson replied, "Me and the old woman walked in, the kids was born there."

About a mile west of Dodson Ranch, the trail crosses Fresno Creek. The Elephant Tusk Trail junction is 0.3 mile west of Fresno Creek. About 1.3 miles farther west the Dodson Trail crosses a high pass, elevation 5,250 feet, then drops into the Smoky Creek drainage.

The trail follows the Smoky Creek drainage for about a mile before exiting on the northwest side of the wash. Watch carefully for large rock cairns on the bank of the wash that mark the junction; many hikers miss this exit and find themselves heading south on the Smoky Creek Trail. If you come to a man-made rock dam in the Smoky Creek wash, you have missed the exit and should backtrack to the Dodson Trail junction.

Dodson; Blue Creek

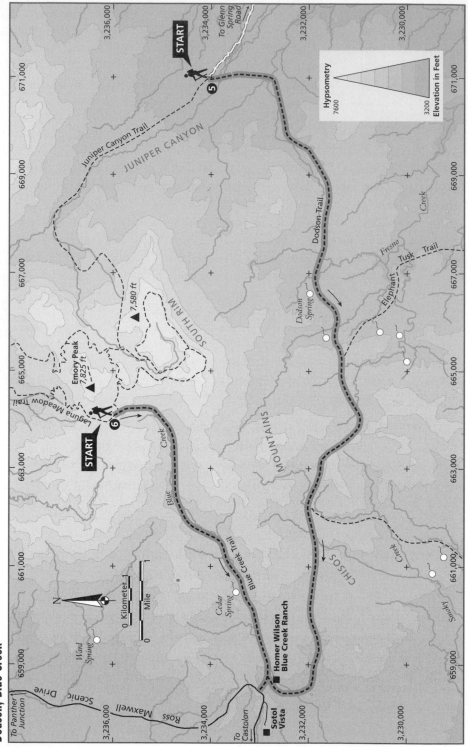

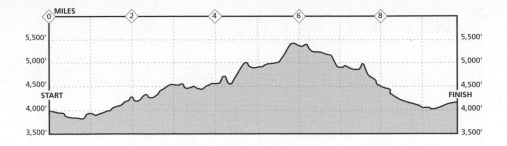

West of the Smoky Creek Trail junction, the Dodson Trail is relatively easy to follow to its end at Homer Wilson Blue Creek Ranch. Hikers wishing to continue up into the Chisos Mountains via the Blue Creek Trail will find the trail intersection at the Homer Wilson Blue Creek Ranch house. Others will end their hike by taking the heavily used, 0.25-mile trail up out of Blue Creek to the Ross Maxwell Scenic Drive.

Miles and Directions

0.0 Trailhead at end of Juniper Canyon Road.

3.6 Dodson Ranch.

4.4 Fresno Creek.

4.7 Elephant Tusk Trail junction.

6.0 High pass—highest point of Dodson Trail, 5,250 feet.

7.1 Smoky Creek Trail junction.

9.9 Homer Wilson Blue Creek Ranch.

6 Blue Creek

General description: A backpack, extended backpack (when combined with other connecting trails), or long day hike, from the wooded Chisos Mountains near Laguna Meadow to the desert grasslands at Homer Wilson Blue Creek Ranch.

Distance: 5.5 miles one way.
Approximate hiking time: 2 to 2.5 hours.
Difficulty: Strenuous.
Traffic: Light.
Trail surface: Dirt path.
Topo map: Emory Peak.

Finding the trailhead: If starting from the Chisos Basin, as this trail description is written, hike up the Laguna Meadow Trail about 3.75 miles to the clearly marked Blue Creek Trail intersection. The Laguna Meadow Trail begins at the west end of the parking lot at the Basin store and visitor center in the Basin. To start at the lower Blue Creek trailhead, follow the Ross Maxwell Scenic Drive about 8.1 miles south of its junction with the Panther Junction-Study Butte highway. A large parking pullout on the left marks the Homer Wilson Blue Creek Ranch overlook and trailhead. Walk 0.25 mile down the trail to the Homer Wilson Blue Creek Ranch house, visible below. The trail starts up the canyon as directed by the sign near the ranch house.

The Hike

If you are hiking only one way, the trail is best done by starting at the Basin and arranging for a shuttle or pick-up at the Homer Wilson Blue Creek Ranch overlook on the Ross Maxwell Scenic Drive. This makes a total hike of 9.5 miles. Many hikers walk this route as one leg of the Outer Mountain Loop, although most of these people will be hiking up the Blue Creek Trail rather than down. The Outer Mountain Loop includes the Blue Creek, Dodson, and Juniper Canyon Trails.

The Blue Creek Trail offers plenty of variety; it begins in mountain woodland and descends through open grasslands before dropping into a rocky creekbed. The upper part of the Blue Creek Trail is rocky, narrow, and steep; good hiking boots are a must. After leaving the Laguna Meadow Trail, you will immediately pass campsites BL 2 and BL 1. You next ascend a small ridge, then start the long downhill into the Blue Creek drainage. Partway into the canyon you will pass the zone camping boundary marked by a sign. Campers with backcountry permits should make their camps only below this sign.

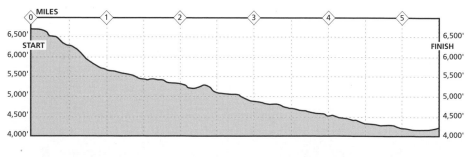

Scars of the 1989 Blue Creek Fire mark the first part of the trail. This human-caused fire burned 331 acres before being contained by Big Bend firefighters working in conjunction with a team of highly trained firefighters from New Mexico. For the first 2 miles or so, the trail passes through the heart of the burn. Charred trees stand as obvious reminders of the blaze. Today the hillside is very open and sunny with scattered pinyon pine, oak, juniper, and various grasses.

The trail drops quite steeply in places as it descends into the drainage. After about an hour of hiking, most hikers will reach the canyon bottom. As you hike through shady oak and juniper groves, you will get a sense of the history of the place. Careful observers will spot the remnants of old fences, a water line, a well, and a watering trough. Homer Wilson, who owned the land as part of his ranch prior to the establishment of Big Bend National Park in 1944, used this trail to move sheep from their winter range in the lowlands up to the cooler Chisos Mountains in summer.

Eventually, the trail emerges from the shadier part of the drainage into a drier, more open canyon bottom. Vegetation becomes smaller and more scrubby, consisting of evergreen sumac, whitethorn acacia, and sotol. The trail winds back and forth across the wash for most of the remainder of the hike, so be sure to watch carefully for the rock cairns that mark exits from the wash.

After about 3.5 miles, the trail enters a section sometimes known as Red Rocks Canyon, a part of Blue Creek Canyon marked by a series of impressive rusty red and white pinnacles that continue for nearly 0.75 mile. Here the trail surface becomes gravelly rather than rocky. As you emerge from the Red Rocks section, you will see the opening of Santa Elena Canyon far to the southwest. You will also see the roof of the partially restored Homer Wilson Blue Creek Ranch house, a former line camp of the old Homer Wilson Ranch. The house marks the end of the hike; from there a 0.25-mile connecting trail climbs up the hillside to the right to the Homer Wilson Blue Creek Ranch overlook and the Ross Maxwell Scenic Drive. The Dodson Trail also begins at the ranch house and continues south down Blue Creek Canyon.

Miles and Directions

0.0   Junction of Blue Creek and Laguna Meadow Trails.

3.5   Red Rocks section of trail.

5.5   Homer Wilson Blue Creek Ranch house.

7 Window View

General description: An introductory day hike that winds through a mountain grassland to a spectacular view of the Window.

Distance: 0.25 mile loop.

Approximate hiking time: 30 minutes.

Difficulty: Very easy; barrier-free.

Traffic: Heavy.

Trail surface: Paved.

Topo map: The Basin.

Finding the trailhead: The trail starts in the Basin at the main trailhead located near the Basin store, visitor center, and lodge.

From the store, follow the sidewalk downhill to the west to the MAIN TRAILHEAD sign.

The Hike

This easy, paved walk winds through a mountain grassland to a spectacular view of the Window. The pinyon pine, juniper, and oak passed along the way once extended across the desert and down to the Rio Grande. Climatic changes during the last 15,000 years caused the area to become warmer and drier, leaving forests only at higher elevations where they can still survive because of additional moisture and cooler temperatures found there.

About halfway along the trail you encounter a plaque commemorating Stephen T. Mather. An influential and wealthy Chicago industrial leader, Mather served as the first director of the National Park Service from 1917 to 1929. He led the drive establishing the National Park Service, formulated policy, and developed the organization required to manage the national park system.

At the midpoint, relax on a bench and enjoy the view of the Window, the V-shaped opening in the mountains on the western horizon. Precipitation falling in the Basin drains through the Window to the desert below. Because no reliable water source exists in the Basin, all potable water for the Basin's visitor facilities comes from Oak Spring in the desert below the Window. Large pumps push the water 1,500 feet higher in elevation via a pipeline through the Window to the Basin development. Because water is such a scarce commodity at Big Bend, be sure to use it wisely during your visit.

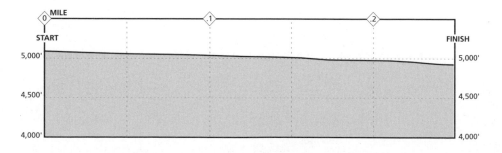

Window View; Window

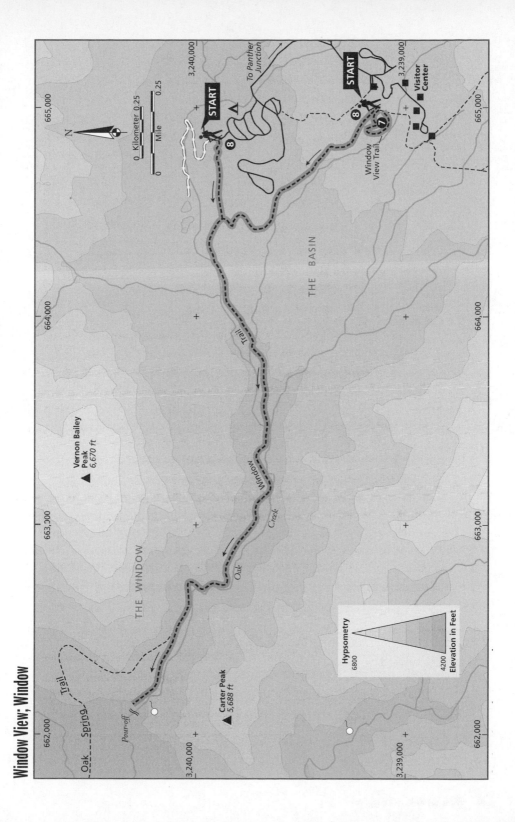

Mist creeps into the Basin through the Window.

Parts of the towns of Study Butte and Terlingua can be seen in the distance through the Window. On a clear day, peaks in Big Bend Ranch State Park and the Sierra Rica of Mexico stand visible on the horizon, 35 miles away. The view covers a broad sweep of the vast terrain of the Big Bend. At sunset, the walk offers one of the best sights in Texas. Clouds light up gold, scarlet, and orange as the sun sinks below the horizon. As the colors fade into dusk, the distant lights of Terlingua and Study Butte blink into life, welcoming cool night.

Miles and Directions

0.0   Basin trailhead.

0.25 End of loop at Basin trailhead.

8 Window

General description: A day hike from the main Basin trailhead to the Window in the Chisos Mountains or a day hike from the Basin Campground.
Distance: 2.8 miles one way, or 2.2 miles one way.

Approximate hiking time: 1 to 1.5 hours.
Difficulty: Moderate.
Traffic: Heavy.
Trail surface: Dirt path.
Topo map: The Basin.

Finding the trailhead: The trail starts in the Basin at the main trailhead located near the Basin store, visitor center, and lodge. From the store, follow the sidewalk downhill to the west to the main trailhead sign. Alternatively, the hike can be started at the trailhead between campsites 49 and 51 in the lower loop of the Basin Campground. Because parking is limited in the campground loop, park in the amphitheater lot across the road from the campground and follow the Window Trail signs through the campground to the trailhead.

The Hike

The Window Trail leads to the Window, a large rock canyon cutting through the Chisos Mountains rim that allows drainage from the Basin. It frames panoramic desert vistas and enhances spectacular scarlet sunsets. The hike offers good wildlife viewing opportunities and an introduction to the geology and plant life of the Chisos Mountains, along with great mountain scenery. Near the end of the Window Trail, a side trail that goes to Oak Spring leads 0.25 mile to a high perch offering outstanding views of the desert far below. The hike is pleasant most of the year. Summers can be fairly hot, so the hike is usually most comfortable in early morning or late afternoon at that time of year. As with other Big Bend hikes, take water, a hat, and sunscreen.

The well-maintained trail descends for its entire length, sometimes fairly steeply in the upper sections. Remember, it may be easy to hike down to the Window, but the return requires a significant climb. The last 0.25 mile or so of the trail lies in a slickrock canyon where footing becomes more difficult. There are rock steps, wet slippery surfaces, and sometimes a short wade across a seasonal creek.

From the main Basin trailhead, the trail begins descending almost immediately, passing through scattered oaks, pines, and junipers. A little more than 0.5 mile down the trail, a spur on the right goes to the campground trailhead. The trail heads west from the spur, traversing the Basin, an eroded bowl that lies some 2,500 feet below the surrounding peaks. Discoveries of Indian artifacts, refuse heaps, baking pits, campsites, and rock art indicate sporadic human occupation in the Basin for thousands of years. Early ranching pioneers used the slopes of the Basin for grazing livestock.

Volcanoes and underground igneous activity created the peaks surrounding the Basin. Beginning about 38 million years ago, two volcanoes spewed vast quantities

Oak Creek flows over polished rock before tumbling over the Window Pour-off.

of ash and lava, while underneath, molten rock squeezed into the bedrock from below, causing the ancestral Chisos Mountains to rise.

After eons of erosion, the resistant rhyolite magma intrusions remain as Ward Mountain, Carter Peak (the sharply pointed peak on the Window's left side), Vernon Bailey Peak (the rounded mountain on the Window's right), and Pulliam Bluff. Towering Casa Grande, Toll Mountain, and Emory Peak, opposite the Window, consist of lava flows and ash beds. Water, wind, heat, and cold have weathered the heavily fissured ridges surrounding the Basin into distinctive pinnacles, spires, and the famous silhouette of the Window.

After a fairly open stretch of about 1 mile or so, the trail reaches wooded Oak Creek. Be sure to watch closely for wildlife in the underbrush. The small Sierra del Carmen white-tailed deer browse on and off throughout the day, while the pig-like collared peccary, or javelina, roots and forages for succulent vegetation. Look for rock squirrels on steep rock faces stashing acorns and pine nuts. Your chance of seeing a gray fox, ringtail, or even a mountain lion improves in the evening or early morning. Black bears are fairly common in this area, especially in the fall when they feed on nuts of the Mexican pinyon pine.

The combination of cacti and century plants, more characteristic of the desert, growing near oak trees, evergreen sumac, and other mountain species may seem odd. However, at the end of the most recent glacial period, a cool, moist climate was replaced by today's warmer and drier conditions. Consequently, desert-adapted plants have taken over the park's lower elevations and infiltrated partway into the mountains. Species adapted to the former climatic conditions withdrew to the cooler, moister, and more hospitable mountains. Pines, oaks, and junipers that once lived at lower altitude have now become dominant plants in the Basin and higher. Look for several of these relict species, or holdovers from the past, including the Mexican drooping juniper and Mexican pinyon pine, along the trail. You may see other distinctive mountain plants, including Texas madrone, mountain mahogany, mountain sage, Mexican buckeye, evergreen sumac, and palo prieto, also known as vauquelinia.

As the trail descends, it leaves the Basin and enters a narrow rock canyon formed by Oak Creek as it carved its way through the Window. Depending on rainfall, a spring sometimes surfaces in the canyon bottom and creates a small flowing stream. Near the end of the trail, the Oak Spring Trail forks off to the right. It climbs above the pour-off, giving great desert views in about 0.25 mile. It then descends around the pour-off to Oak Spring and beyond. Soon after passing the junction, the improved dirt trail ends. Beyond here, the trail follows sections of bare rock and stone steps a short distance down to the trail's end at the top of the Window Pour-off. If rainfall has been adequate, a small stream tumbles down over small cascades through a polished rock course alongside the trail. Do not approach the top of the pour-off too closely; slippery, wet rocks make footing treacherous. A fall would be fatal.

As the only drainage system for the Basin, Oak Creek and its tributaries channel all rain and snowmelt through the Window, the sole gap in the Basin rim. Although the Basin receives only about 15 inches of precipitation annually, summer thundershowers can turn the rock gorge at the end of the Window Trail into a raging torrent in less than an hour. Rushing water carries pebbles and debris through this narrow defile to plummet 220 feet over the Window Pour-off to the desert below. Be wary here during stormy weather; a flash flood could also wash you over the lip. As the years go by, storms will continue to scour the slopes of the Basin, eroding it deeper and deeper.

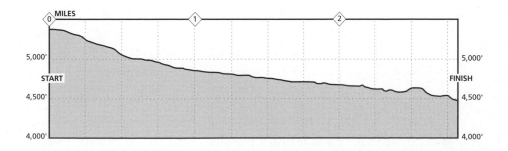

Miles and Directions

0.0 Basin trailhead.

0.7 Campground spur trail junction. Stay left and continue downhill.

2.3 Oak Spring Trail junction. Stay left, downstream.

2.8 Window Pour-off.

9 Lost Mine

General description: A day hike to high mountain overlooks with some of the best views in the park.
Distance: 2.4 miles one way.
Approximate hiking time: 1 to 1.5 hours.

Difficulty: Moderately strenuous.
Traffic: Heavy.
Trail surface: Dirt path.
Topo map: The Basin.

Finding the trailhead: From Panther Junction, drive 3 miles west toward Study Butte. Turn left onto the Basin road and drive 5.4 miles to the large parking area on the left at Panther Pass.

The Hike

The Lost Mine Trail is one of the most popular in the park. Most hikers in good shape can do the round trip in three to four hours. For those without the time to hike to the South Rim, this trail is an excellent substitute. People with even less time or energy may elect to hike only the relatively easy first mile of the trail; on clear days this provides beautiful views of Juniper Canyon and south into Mexico. A self-guiding booklet for this trail can be obtained from a box at the trailhead; numbered posts along the route match the guide.

Between 1940 and 1942, Civilian Conservation Corps (CCC) crews built this trail for the new Big Bend National Park, authorized in 1935 and established in 1944. Look for evidence of their skilled craftsmanship in the stonework of the old walls and culverts found along the path. The surface of the Lost Mine Trail is rocky and well-worn with rock and log water bars scattered along the route. Water bars are small ridges built across the trail that channel water off the trail to limit erosion.

From the parking area, the trail ascends gradually through juniper, oak, and pinyon pine forest along the base of Casa Grande Peak. Do not let the steep first 100 feet or so scare you away. At about 1 mile, the trail reaches a saddle that looks out over Juniper Canyon and far south into Mexico. From this vantage point, you will have views of Casa Grande to the west, and Toll Mountain and the Northeast Rim of the Chisos to the south and southwest.

Listen for the loud, raucous call of the gray-breasted jay; you might see a flash of bright blue as it flies across your path. This is also a good place for the tufted tit-

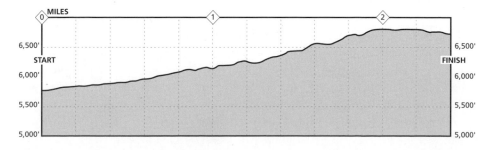

Broad views of mountain and desert reward hikers at the end of the Lost Mine Trail.

mouse, a small, crested bird whose plaintive call of "peter, peter, peter" is easily identified.

After the saddle, the trail climbs more steeply up a few switchbacks then flattens out temporarily on an open hillside of stipa grass, pinyon pine, and juniper. The trail quickly begins climbing steeply again. Views of Juniper Canyon continue. The trail then narrows, and woods of pinyon pine and oak close in. More switchbacks rapidly add elevation, and good views resume to the south and west. In the midst of the switchbacks you can look west and see the Chisos Basin Campground and the Window.

On the last couple of switchbacks, the trail gets very steep and rocky. Log and rock steps and exposed bedrock in this stretch can be slippery if wet. To most hikers' relief, the trail abruptly levels off at the top of the ridge. Most of the last 0.5 mile along the exposed ridge is easy. Walk all the way to the end for the best views of Pine Canyon (below, to the left) and the Sierra del Carmen in Mexico (on the eastern horizon). On the right, sheer cliffs tumble down into Juniper Canyon, far below. The East Rim of the Chisos Mountains towers over the far side of the broad canyon,

Lost Mine; Pine Canyon

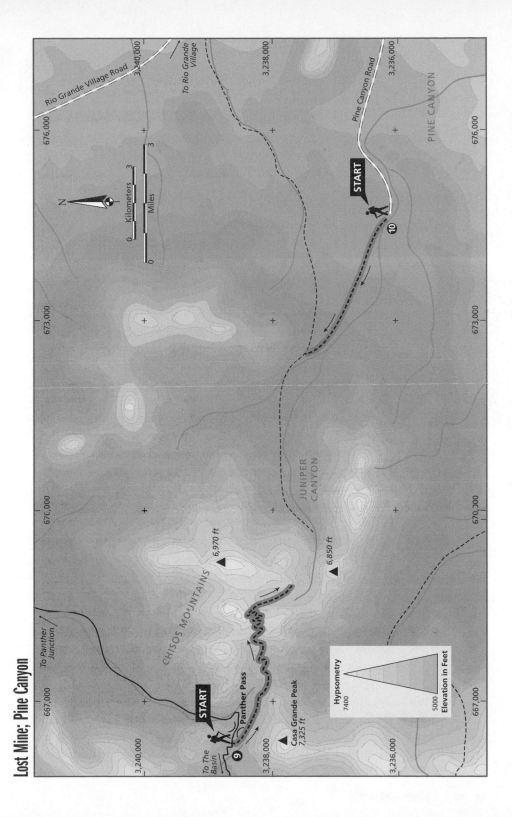

and the distinctive pointed summit of Elephant Tusk rises above the desert to the south.

Just northeast, across Pine Canyon, lies Lost Mine Peak, one of the highest summits in the Chisos. The peak was named for an old legend. Supposedly, at certain times of the year, the rising sun shines on the entrance of a rich mine developed by the old Spaniards. Unfortunately, the Chisos Mountains are not geologically predisposed to such mineralization, making the legend probably little more than a fanciful story. The treasures here are more spiritual than material.

Miles and Directions

0.0   Panther Pass trailhead.
0.8   Juniper Canyon overlook.
2.4   End of trail.

10 Pine Canyon

General description: A day hike through a sotol grassland into a shaded Chisos Mountains canyon.
Distance: 2 miles one way.
Approximate hiking time: 1 hour.

Difficulty: Moderate.
Traffic: Moderate.
Trail surface: Dirt path.
Topo maps: Panther Junction, The Basin.

Finding the trailhead: From park headquarters at Panther Junction, take the road to Rio Grande Village. About 5 miles down the road, turn right onto the dirt Glenn Spring Road. After following this road for about 2 miles, turn right onto Pine Canyon Road. Follow it to the trailhead at its end. A high-clearance vehicle is usually needed for Glenn Spring and Pine Canyon Roads. Check on road conditions at park headquarters before you begin.

The Hike

This trail provides expansive views of high desert grasslands and the drier desert below before leading into a densely wooded canyon of the Chisos Mountains. Because Lloyd Wade once had a ranch here, the canyon was called Wade Canyon at one time. The trail crosses part of an ancient collapsed volcano, or caldera. The hike is hot in summer, but still considerably cooler than the desert lowlands. Get an early start during the warm months of the year and carry lots of water. Plenty of shade on the last 0.6 mile of the hike makes the hike pleasant even on hot days.

The trail follows an old dirt road, a continuation of Pine Canyon Road, steadily uphill through a sotol-dotted grassland. The canyon narrows as you climb to the west toward the mountains. The old road ends as the trail turns toward the south-

Chisos Mountains.

west and enters a more narrow and sheltered section of Pine Canyon. The path enters thick woodland and winds among oaks, junipers, pinyon pines, and even Arizona pines. Texas madrones, smooth white to pinkish barked evergreen trees, are common in this protected canyon. Reduced exposure to sun and wind allows trees and other plants to thrive here.

The trail climbs steadily up the canyon and ends at the base of a 200-foot-high pour-off, a waterfall after heavy rains. There is often at least some dripping water here. This is one of the few places in the park where columbine, a beautiful yellow-flowered plant, grows, so be careful not to step on vegetation in the pour-off area. Relax in the shade and enjoy one of the most lush areas in the park. Because the canyon is small and delicate, camping is not allowed here.

Miles and Directions

0.0 Trailhead. Trail follows old dirt road west toward mountains.

1.4 Trail enters shaded canyon where old road ends.

2.0 Trail ends at base of pour-off.

11 Oak Spring

General description: A day hike past a high seasonal waterfall at the Window to a connection with the Window Trail.

Distance: 2 miles one way.

Approximate hiking time: 1 hour.

Difficulty: Moderate.

Traffic: Moderate.

Trail surface: Dirt path.

Topo map: The Basin.

Finding the trailhead: From the Santa Elena Junction about 13 miles west of Panther Junction on the road to Study Butte and Alpine, turn south onto the Ross Maxwell Scenic Drive toward Castolon and Santa Elena Canyon. Turn left onto the dirt road across from the Sam Nail Ranch paved parking pullout on the right after 3.4 miles. Follow the rough dirt road 1.3 miles to a parking area; a gate blocks the road beyond the lot. If great care is used and rains have not roughed up the road, most cars can make it to the parking lot. However, a high-clearance vehicle is preferable. To save wear and tear on your car, you may wish to hike this trail as an extension of the Window Trail, in reverse order from the description below. The Window Trail starts at the west side of the large parking lot at the store and visitor center in the Basin.

The Hike

Oak Spring lies below the Window, a rocky gap in the west side of the Chisos Mountains that drains the large inner valley of the Basin. The rugged crags of Carter and Vernon Bailey Peaks rise above the narrow defile like ancient guard towers. Depending on rainfall, a small stream sometimes tumbles down through the Window, culminating at the Window Pour-off in a 220-foot cascade, one of the tallest waterfalls in Texas. Downstream lies Oak Spring, the Basin water supply. This hike goes by both the spring and the pour-off.

The Window Trail leads to the upper trailhead of the Oak Spring Trail. Using this approach, you reach the upper end of the Oak Spring Trail near the end of the Window Trail. The upper third of the Oak Spring Trail is the most spectacular section, especially when combined with the Window Trail. However, to help people find the lower trailhead, this description will describe the hike starting from the bottom and continuing to the upper trailhead at the junction with the Window Trail. Regardless of which trailhead you use, the trail is easily followed, although it is quite steep and rocky in sections.

To start this hike, continue up the road beyond the gate toward the mountains above. In about 0.5 mile, the road crosses Oak Creek. A small stream usually flows across the road, fed by Oak Spring a short distance upstream. As in other isolated spots in the Big Bend desert, the water creates a lush oasis that hugs the stream banks. A dense woodland of willows, oaks, cottonwoods, and other trees creates a welcome canopy of shade at the creek crossing. Many birds twitter in the foliage, taking advantage of the extra moisture, food, and shelter. Careful inspection will

A hiker relaxes at a "tie-down tree" by Oak Creek.

often reveal tracks of animals such as deer, ringtails, and javelina in the damp earth on the stream banks.

The main trunk of a large oak arches over almost horizontal to the ground at the crossing. Legend says the oak is a "tie-down tree," bent over by Comanches or other Indians as a marker of some sort. Regardless, the bent-over trunk provides a great rest spot on a hot day.

From the tree, cross the creek and continue along the road on the other side. The vegetation reverts to cacti, desert scrub, and dry grasses as soon as the road leaves the creek. A short distance up the road, the marked trail turns left off the road. The road continues only a short distance farther, ending at a large water tank and pump system. The facility pumps water taken from Oak Spring up a pipeline through the Window to park and concession facilities in the Basin. The trail follows the pipeline route some of the time.

The trail climbs steadily up toward the Window across a bench high above Oak Creek. A view opens up of the tall cascade that sometimes pours down through the Window. Although it may be tempting to climb down to the base of the waterfall, the descent is a steep, hazardous scramble on loose rock. Use care if you attempt it.

Oak Spring

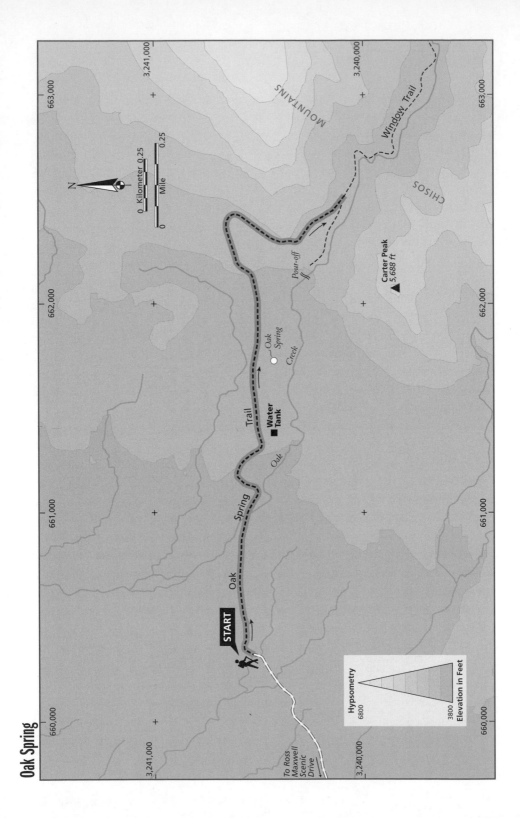

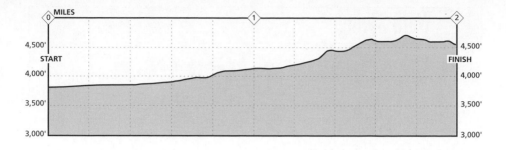

The trail steepens as it switchbacks up the steep slope to the left of the tall cliffs that frame the left side of the Window. The trail eventually tops out then descends a short distance to the junction with the Window Trail along Oak Creek above the pour-off. From there, you can return the same way or follow the Window Trail a short way down Oak Creek to its end at the top of the pour-off.

With a shuttle arrangement, you can also continue up the Window Trail to the lodge or campground areas in the Basin.

Miles and Directions

0.0 Trailhead parking area.

0.5 Trail (dirt road) crosses Oak Creek.

0.8 Route leaves dirt road and starts up trail.

1.2 View of Window Pour-off seasonal waterfall.

2.0 Trail joins Window Trail.

12 Ward Spring

General description: A day hike to a spring in the Chisos Mountains foothills once used as a water source for livestock.
Distance: 1.8 miles one way.
Approximate hiking time: 1 hour.

Difficulty: Moderate.
Traffic: Light.
Trail surface: Dirt path.
Topo map: Emory Peak.

Finding the trailhead: From the Santa Elena Junction about 13 miles west of Panther Junction on the road to Study Butte and Alpine, drive south on the Ross Maxwell Scenic Drive toward Castolon and Santa Elena Canyon. The trailhead lies at the paved pullout on the left after 5.6 miles.

The Hike

The lightly used Ward Spring Trail is a relatively easy trail physically, but requires some modest route-finding ability, earning it a moderate difficulty rating. Most maps do not show the trail. It starts in the western foothills of the Chisos Mountains near the east edge of Burro Mesa. It climbs gradually but steadily to a spring at the base of the high ramparts of the upper Chisos Mountains.

Sharp eyes can sometimes pick out the spring east of the parking lot at a low point in a large igneous dike cut through by Cottonwood Creek. The dike trends roughly north–south across the flanks of the Chisos Mountains. The hard, impermeable rock of the dike forces water flowing underground in creek gravels to the surface where it crosses the dike. The green glint of trees growing at the spring is just barely visible from the trailhead.

The igneous dikes in the Ward Spring area formed when molten rock squeezed into vertical cracks in rock layers beneath the surface and solidified. Because the rock layers were softer than the dike material, they eroded first, leaving dikes standing above the surface like Chinese walls.

Ward Spring is not correctly marked on the Emory Peak topographic map. It lies on Cottonwood Creek about 0.3 mile north of where it is marked on the map. It is located about where the "C" of Creek (from Cottonwood Creek) is lettered on the map. The Trails Illustrated Big Bend National Park map shows it more correctly, although a bit upstream of the dike. The trail itself is not shown on either map, but it follows a roughly straight line from the highway to the spring.

Ward Spring was once part of the Homer Wilson Ranch on the western slopes of the Chisos Mountains. Thick grasses once blanketed the hills, but overgrazing removed much of the grass cover. Once heavy rains eroded the topsoil, damage

An igneous dike cuts through the hills and helps create Ward Spring. ▶

Ward Spring

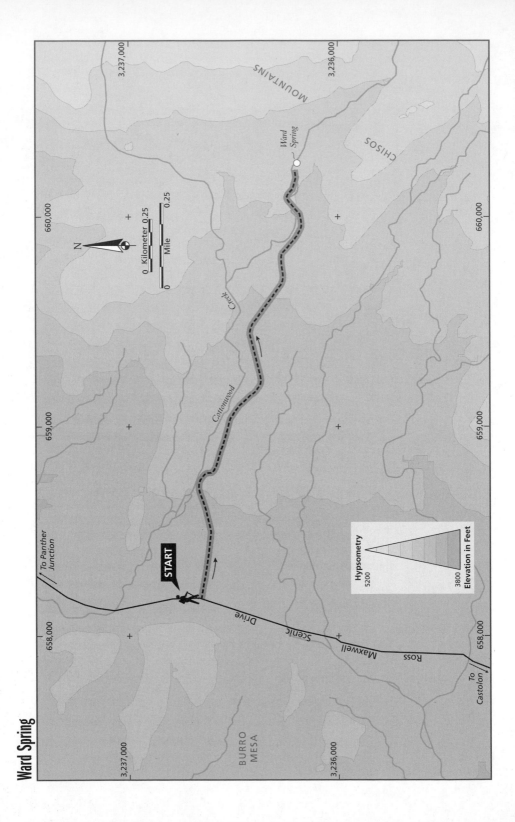

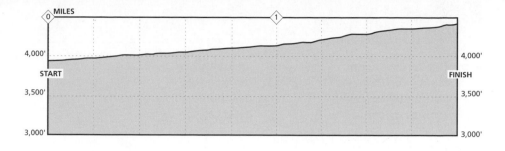

resulted that is taking many years to repair. Grasses have been slowly returning as the land recovers.

Like most park springs, the waters of Ward Spring were used for livestock during the area's ranching days. A pipeline carried water down from the spring to a stock tank north of the parking area. Much of the trail follows the old pipeline route, although the pipe is only occasionally visible.

At the parking area, look for a faint trail heading east toward the mountains. Small rock piles, or cairns, help mark the route to the spring. The trail is relatively faint but generally easy to follow. It climbs steadily, but at a fairly gentle grade for the first mile or so. Watch closely for the trail right after the first piece of the old pipeline is visible; it gets faint for a short distance. The pipeline appears periodically after that point. As the trail gets close to the steep mountain slopes, it too begins to climb more steeply and passes through a few short but sharp ups and downs.

After you crest a small rise, trees fed by the spring are easily visible in the drainage below the dike and make the destination clear. The trail drops into the creek bottom and remains there the rest of the 0.25 mile or so to the spring. Rocks and brush make the route up the creek bottom more difficult, but cairns help mark the easiest way. The trail soon hits trees such as willows and walnuts, and, depending on rainfall, water. The heart of the spring is where the creek crosses the large dike visible from the highway. Relax and enjoy the shady spot beneath the towering ramparts of the Chisos Mountains.

Except during extended droughts, the spring runs year-round, but plan to carry plenty of water just in case. If water is taken from the spring, it should be purified.

Miles and Directions

0.0 Ward Spring trailhead.

1.8 Ward Spring.

13 Sam Nail Ranch

General description: An easy walk through an old ranch site below Burro Mesa.
Distance: 0.5 mile loop.
Approximate hiking time: 30 minutes.

Difficulty: Easy.
Traffic: Heavy.
Trail surface: Dirt path.
Topo map: The Basin.

Finding the trailhead: From the Santa Elena Junction about 13 miles west of Panther Junction on the road to Study Butte and Alpine, drive south on the Ross Maxwell Scenic Drive toward Castolon and Santa Elena Canyon. The trailhead lies at the large paved pullout on the right after 3.4 miles.

The Hike

This short, well-maintained trail loops through the old Sam Nail Ranch site. Sam Nail and his younger brother, Jim, moved to the valley between the western slope of the Chisos Mountains and Burro Mesa in 1916. With little outside help, they dug a well and built a one-story adobe house above Cottonwood Creek at the base of Burro Mesa. The home had a concrete floor, wooden viga-and-cane ceiling, and sheet metal roof. With milk cows, chickens, cattle, a garden, and fruit trees, they were relatively self-sufficient. In 1918, Sam married Nena Burnam, whose family lived nearby at Government Spring.

The Nails owned several sections and leased more for their ranching activities. After they left, nature began to reclaim the site. Rains have slowly melted away much of the soft adobe walls of the house, and desert plants have taken over the yard and garden. The park still maintains a windmill at the ranch; its waters maintain a tiny oasis of walnuts, pecans, willows, and even a fig tree.

The trail heads west, slightly downhill, from the parking lot and forks into a loop in 100 yards or so. Go right and pass an old ruined windmill in a short distance. The trail then drops down into a thicket of small trees in the floodplain of Cottonwood Creek. A very short, unofficial side trail on the right leads to an old chicken coop and the creek. A few cottonwoods line the creek, where small amounts of water sometimes flow, depending on rainfall.

From the thicket, the main trail leads into a grove of larger trees surrounding the working windmill. The wind slowly pumps up a small flow of water that nourishes the surrounding trees and plants. Even such a small flow makes a tremendous biological difference in such dry desert country. Relax on a bench in the cool shade and listen to the sounds of the creaking windmill mixed with plentiful birdcalls. You may see cardinals, summer tanagers, house finches, mockingbirds, varied buntings, and many other species.

From the windmill, continue around the loop on the main trail. Resist the urge to take a shortcut by the windmill to the old house ruins in this heavily visited spot.

Sam Nail Ranch

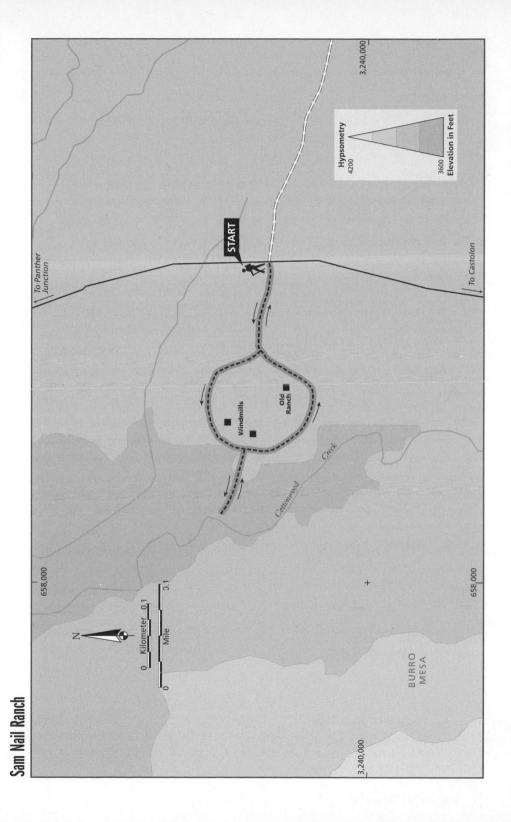

An old windmill still stands at the Sam Nail Ranch site.

The old adobe walls of the ranch house lie on the left only a short distance up the hill on the main trail. From the old house, continue the rest of the way around the loop back to the parking lot.

Miles and Directions

0.0 Sam Nail Ranch parking area.

0.25 Working windmill.

0.5 Sam Nail Ranch parking area.

14 Burro Mesa Pour-off

General description: A hike to a seasonal waterfall at the southern end of Burro Mesa.
Distance: 0.5 mile one way.
Approximate hiking time: 30 minutes.

Difficulty: Easy.
Traffic: Heavy.
Trail surface: Dirt path.
Topo map: Cerro Castellan.

Finding the trailhead: From the Panther Junction Visitor Center, go west on the park road toward Study Butte and Alpine. Travel about 13 miles to the junction of the road to Santa Elena Canyon and turn left onto the Ross Maxwell Scenic Drive. Note that on your right is Burro Mesa and to your left are the Chisos Mountains. Travel south about 11.5 miles and turn right onto the Burro Mesa spur road. Follow the spur road to its end (1.8 miles). The trailhead is located at the end of the road.

The Hike

This short trail to a desert pour-off offers much to hikers interested in the geology of Big Bend. To give some perspective, recall the view of the high, rugged peaks of the Chisos Mountains as you drove down to Burro Mesa. The rock exposed in the cliffs here is the same as is found on the top of Emory Peak, the highest point in the park. Burro Mesa is a down-faulted block, a large landmass that dropped along a fault line approximately 26 million years ago. The extent of the displacement is more than 3,000 feet.

Before starting down the trail, hikers should take a moment to look at the rock section exposed in the canyon wall to the left. The darker volcanic rock at the top of the canyon is Burro Mesa rhyolite. The thick yellow band beneath it is the Wasp Spring flow breccia. Both of these are members of the South Rim Formation. Underlying the breccia member is an unnamed conglomerate, large boulders of which will be found along the trail. The tall, white formation exposed to the right of the trail is volcanic tuff (consolidated ash) of the Chisos Formation.

The first portion of the trail is a well-defined path into the canyon. You first hike to the top of a short slope where the trail descends into a dry wash. By looking up into the canyon ahead you can see a small pour-off. This is not the final destination, however. Follow the trail down into and across the wash. The trail passes through a dense thicket of guayacan and enters the dry wash again. At this point the trail is no longer a well-defined path. A line of rocks directs hikers into the drainage opening to the right. Continuing

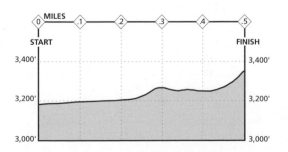

up this gravel-floored wash, you pass several healthy stands of Texas persimmon, which in late summer can be filled with small black persimmons and large wasps feasting on them. About halfway up the wash on the right, a large Mexican buckeye offers hikers a shady spot to sit and rest. Beyond this point, the wash continues up the canyon and turns to the left. The Burro Mesa Pour-off comes into view, high above.

The pour-off is a long, narrow chute that drains Javelina Wash from the canyon in the cliffs above. The dark, polished rock that is exposed for most of the length of the chute is Burro Mesa rhyolite. The contact between the rhyolite and the Wasp Spring breccia is seen quite easily in the ledges just above your head. Usually the chute is dry, but the extent of the cut testifies to the powerful torrent of water that can be generated after heavy summer rains fall on the upper reaches of Burro Mesa and the western slopes of the Chisos Mountains.

Do not try to climb up to the pour-off. Cliffs and steep slopes with loose rubble make ascents hazardous. Although this walk is short, it can be very hot in summer. Plan to hike it early in the day during the warm months. Be wary of flooding during and after heavy rains.

Miles and Directions

0.0 Trailhead.

0.1 Trail descends into and crosses dry wash.

0.2 Trail enters wash again. Follow rock alignment into drainage to right and follow wash upstream to pour-off.

0.5 Pour-off.

◀ *An easy trail up a dry wash leads to the Burro Mesa Pour-off.*

Burro Mesa Pour-off; Top of Burro Mesa Pour-off; Burro Spring

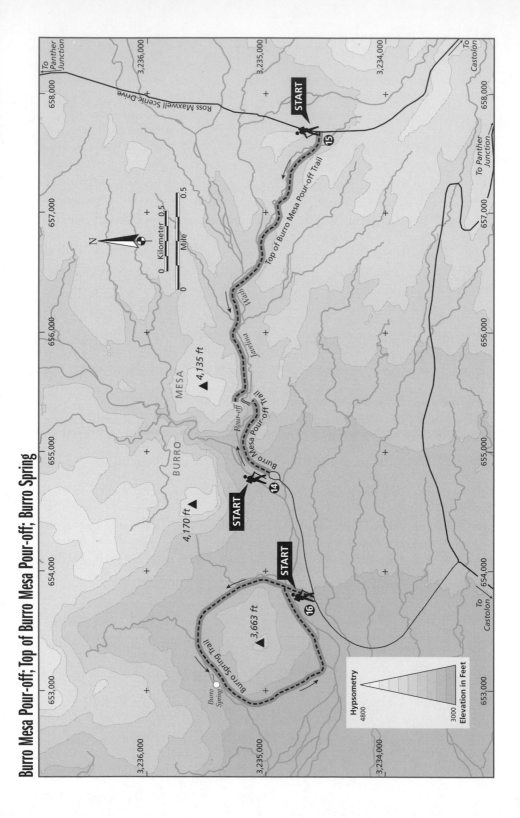

15 Top of Burro Mesa Pour-off

General description: A hike through some narrow, rocky gorges to the lip of a high, dry waterfall.

Distance: 1.8 miles one way.

Approximate hiking time: 1 hour one way.

Difficulty: Moderate.

Traffic: Light.

Trail surface: Dirt path and sand, gravel, and cobbles of dry desert wash.

Topo map: Cerro Castellan.

Finding the trailhead: From the Santa Elena Junction about 13 miles west of Panther Junction on the road to Study Butte and Alpine, drive south on the Ross Maxwell Scenic Drive toward Castolon and Santa Elena Canyon. The trailhead lies at the paved pullout on the right at about 6.9 miles.

The Hike

The trail to the top of the Burro Mesa Pour-off is relatively easy physically, but does require some route-finding skill. A topographic map and compass would be good insurance for this hike. Most of the hike follows desert washes where there is no formal trail and rock cairns may wash away in floods. Although the route is primitive, most of the walking is easy, except for a few rock scrambles early in the hike. Although canyon walls create some shade, especially toward the end of the hike, this is a very hot walk in summer. Take plenty of water.

The trail trends steadily downward, mostly at a gentle grade, through a series of desert washes all the way to the top of the pour-off. The pour-off is a high, dry desert waterfall that drops precipitously from the canyon that the trail follows into a rugged lower canyon. In flash floods, the waterfall and canyon can become a raging torrent, so this hike should be avoided in stormy weather.

The trail, clearly visible at first, drops down into a small, grassy valley below the parking pullout. It follows the valley downstream a short distance and then drops into a gravel and rock wash. The valley narrows into a rocky canyon, requiring some rock scrambling down the wash. After about 0.75 mile, a large tributary joins the canyon from the right. Note carefully the proper canyon for your return hike. The canyon broadens and the grade lessens below the confluence. Another, even larger

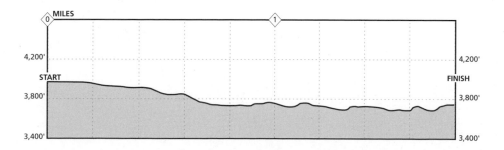

wash, Javelina Wash, joins from the right in another 0.25 mile. Again note your return route. These two side washes are the most likely points of confusion on the return hike. However, if you should take one by accident, it's no problem; they both end up on the highway just north of the trailhead.

After the Javelina Wash confluence, the wash becomes large. Follow it the rest of the way downstream to the pour-off. The canyon walls slowly close in and get higher and higher. Just before the pour-off, the canyon turns into a slot canyon; scenic, but a poor place to be in a flood. At the pour-off, the canyon ends abruptly where it drops off into space. Far below, you may see people hiking up to the base of the pour-off from a lower trail. However, because of the tall cliff, you will need to hike back the same way.

Miles and Directions

0.0 Top of Burro Mesa Pour-off trailhead.

1.0 Trail joins Javelina Wash.

1.8 Top of Burro Mesa Pour-off.

16 Burro Spring

General description: A day hike to a desert spring.
Distance: 2.2-mile loop.
Approximate hiking time: 1 hour (for full loop).

Difficulty: Easy.
Traffic: Light.
Trail surface: Dirt path.
Topo map: Cerro Castellan.

Finding the trailhead: From the Panther Junction Visitor Center, go west on the park road toward Study Butte and Alpine. Drive about 13 miles to the junction of the road to Santa Elena Canyon and turn left onto the Ross Maxwell Scenic Drive. Follow it south about 11.5 miles and turn right onto the Burro Mesa spur road. The trailhead lies on the left side of the spur road, just a little more than 1 mile from the junction.

The Hike

If you want a short hike that gives the feeling of vast isolation written about in Edward Abbey books, this trail is for you. This is a good trail for seeing lizards and insects as well. It is a hot trail in summer; if you hike then, be sure to start early in the day and carry plenty of water.

◀ *The canyon gets narrower as the trail approaches the top of the Burro Mesa Pour-off.*

An easy desert trail leads to Burro Spring.

The trail heads toward the large hill that lies just northwest of the trailhead. It quickly drops into a large wash that drains much of Burro Mesa then follows a smaller left-hand wash tributary as it circles left around the hill. The trail climbs slowly upstream to a low saddle then continues to circle the hill to the west and then southwest above a new drainage that leads to Burro Spring.

Colorful layers of rock tower over low desert scrub along the easy walk. From an overlook, where you can see the tall cottonwoods of Burro Spring below, the trail drops about 100 feet to the spring. Stop and look for wildlife before descending the trail to the spring; you may see deer, javelina, coyote, fox, or even a mountain lion at the spring. Once there, watch for tracks in the wet soil.

From the spring, you can either return on the same trail or continue on a primitive route to circle back around the south side of the hill on your left to the trailhead. It is the same distance either way. To continue on the primitive route, travel left around the hill by following the wash below the spring for maybe 50–100 yards. Climb left out of the wash onto a faint trail following an old roadway that leads southeast. Imagine traveling this road long ago to get water from the spring. Follow

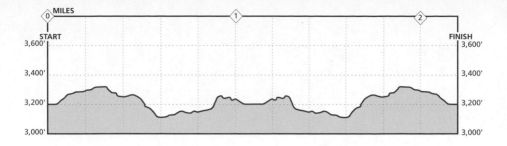

the rocks piled along the faint roadway until you come to a large dry wash. Turn left into the wash to return to the trailhead.

Miles and Directions

0.0 Trailhead.

0.6 High point at saddle.

1.1 Burro Spring.

2.2 Arrive back at the trailhead.

17 The Chimneys

General description: A day hike (or 15.2-mile, round-trip backpack) past a prominent rock landmark to Old Maverick Road.
Distance: 7.6 miles one way.
Approximate hiking time: 3.5 to 4 hours.

Difficulty: Easy one-way, moderate round-trip.
Traffic: Moderate to the Chimneys, light beyond.
Trail surface: Dirt path.
Topo maps: Cerro Castellan, Castolon.

Finding the trailhead: From park headquarters at Panther Junction, go about 13 miles west on the road to Alpine and Study Butte. Turn left onto the paved road to Santa Elena Canyon and Castolon. Go about 12.8 miles to the small parking area on the right (west) side of the road, about 1.3 miles beyond the Burro Mesa spur road. A small sign marks the Chimneys Trail. The western trailhead is at the Chimneys West primitive vehicle campsite near Luna's Jacal on Old Maverick Road.

The Hike

The tall ridge of rock outcrops known as the Chimneys has been a landmark for hundreds of years. Indian petroglyphs decorate one rock wall, and the remains of small rock shelters used by herders are tucked against the rocks.

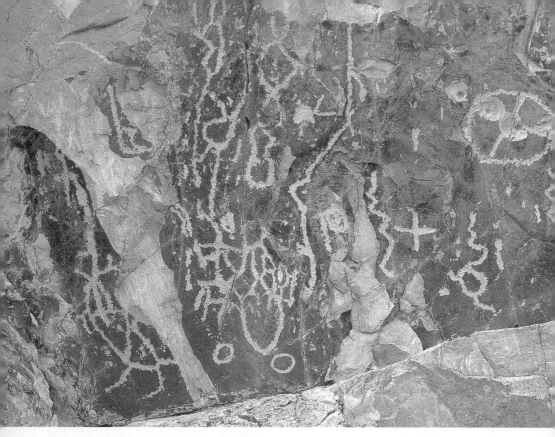

Indian petroglyphs mark a rock at the Chimneys.

This trail is a cool weather hike. Temperatures can begin to get very hot as early as April 1. The Chimneys and Peña Spring have the only shade. Be sure to carry plenty of water; springs are not always reliable, and hikers must purify spring water.

The trail is most easily done as a one-way hike to Old Maverick Road with a shuttle arranged at the other end. Another good option is a round-trip day hike only as far as the Chimneys for a total distance of 4.8 miles. The trail is well traveled and clearly visible as far as the Chimneys; beyond, it is much less used and occasionally gets faint. Topographic maps and a compass would be good insurance. The mileages shown on the current sign at the start of the trail are a touch high.

The Chimneys are visible from the trailhead as a long, rocky ridge down the long slope to the west. They appear closer than the 2.4 miles away that they are. The good, easy trail follows a fairly straight route across the desert flats to the Chimneys. The ridge is in sight for virtually all of the first half of the hike. The trail slopes slightly downhill for the entire route, except for a short, easy climb right near the end. Conversely, almost the entire trail requires a gentle climb on the return trip.

The Chimneys are reached at about 2.4 miles. Erosion has carved a narrow ridge into a series of pinnacles and buttes. Indians carved petroglyphs onto a wall of the

The Chimneys

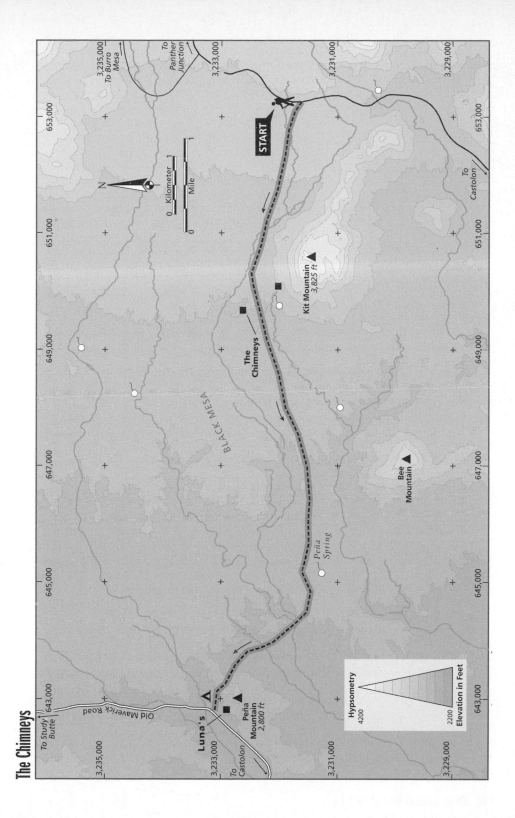

START

The Chimneys

Kit Mountain
3,825 ft

Bee
Mountain

BLACK MESA

Peña Spring

Luna's

Peña Mountain
2,800 ft

Old Maverick Road

To Study Butte

To Castolon

To Castolon

To Panther Junction

To Burro Mesa

N

0   Kilometer   1

0   Mile   1

Hypsometry
4200
2200
Elevation in Feet

3,235,000
3,233,000
3,231,000
3,229,000

653,000
651,000
649,000
647,000
645,000
643,000

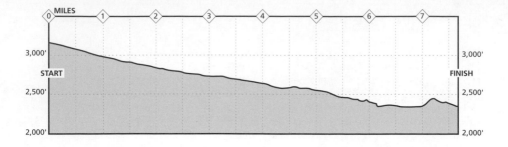

southernmost rock tower. Please don't disturb or deface them. Some rock shelters surround the same tower.

To continue on the Chimneys Trail, follow the main trail west-southwest from between the main Chimneys ridge and the separate southernmost tower. Ignore several unofficial trails that wind around the Chimneys. The route west of the Chimneys is considerably less traveled, but still easy to follow. Rock cairns help guide you. A few trees in a draw just west of the southernmost Chimney mark a small spring. The trail aims roughly at the distant mouth of Santa Elena Canyon for the nearly 3 miles from the Chimneys to Peña Spring. It stays on a flat, gently sloping divide between two drainages for the entire distance.

The trail eventually drops into a shallow ravine marked with willows and cottonwoods. Peña Spring announces itself with the muted tinkle of trickling water. Depending on rainfall, the spring's water sometimes runs down the draw alongside the trail for the next 0.75 mile or so. Watch carefully for the trail as it crisscrosses the draw until it opens up into a broad valley. The trail then turns northwest to cross the upper part of the valley and leaves the small creek behind. It climbs up over a low saddle just north of Peña Mountain, then drops down a small draw to the Chimneys West primitive campsite. Old Maverick Road is just a short distance away along the campsite spur road.

Miles and Directions

0.0 Chimneys trailhead.

2.4 The Chimneys.

5.3 Peña Spring.

7.6 Chimneys West campsite off Old Maverick Road.

18 Mule Ears Peaks

General description: A day hike from the Mule Ears Viewpoint trailhead to the junction with the Smoky Creek Trail.
Distance: 3.5 miles one way.
Approximate hiking time: 1.5 to 2 hours.

Difficulty: Moderate.
Traffic: Light to moderate.
Trail surface: Dirt path.
Topo map: Cerro Castellan.

Finding the trailhead: The Mule Ears trailhead is located at the Mule Ears Viewpoint parking area along the Ross Maxwell Scenic Drive, about 28 miles southwest of Panther Junction.

The Hike

The Mule Ears Trail showcases the unusual beauty of the Chihuahuan Desert. Various cacti and other desert plants border the trail as it winds through dry washes and across rolling desert terrain. During years of plentiful rain, springs and seeps stand out as verdant patches of lush vegetation, where cottonwoods, cattails, and willow trees shade pools inhabited by leopard frogs. As you follow the trail across the desert, enjoy the ever-changing views of Mule Ears Peaks and the southern extension of the Chisos Mountains, the Sierra Quemada (Spanish for "burned mountains").

This is a very hot trail during the warm months of the year. Avoid it in midday in the hot season. Although the trail passes two springs, do not rely on them. Carry plenty of your own drinking water. Note that the USGS topographic map shows the incorrect trail location from east of Mule Ears Spring to Smoky Creek. The Trails Illustrated topographic map shows the trail route correctly. Although the net elevation gain is only about 20 feet for the hike, there is actually about 400 feet of total gain and loss on the route.

The first part of the trail skirts the southern flank of Trap Mountain, a symmetrical peak composed of lava flows deposited some 35 million years ago. The soft, light gray rock underfoot is volcanic ash tuff.

The Mule Ears Peaks and their smaller volcanic brothers were created by differential erosion of lava beds. Small caps of especially hard lava protect the peaks from erosion as the softer surrounding lava erodes away. Interestingly, ancient bones of

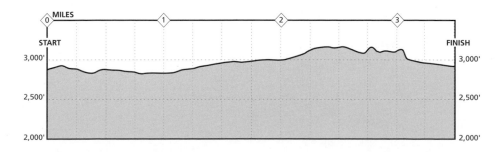

Mule Ears Peaks rise above Smoky Creek.

California condors have been found in a small cave on one of the Mule Ears Peaks, indicating that these nearly extinct birds once ranged to the Big Bend country.

Mule Ears Spring is a popular destination for many people, and the extra effort of hiking another mile is rewarded with good views of the Sierra Quemada, Smoky Creek, and the eastern side of the Mule Ears Peaks. From Mule Ears Spring, the trail climbs out of one drainage, over a low divide, and into another drainage. It then climbs onto a low ridge, or escarpment, overlooking the broad valley of Smoky Creek. The trail then drops to the Smoky Creek Trail. Remember that east of Mule Ears Spring, the trail follows a route different than that marked on the USGS 7.5-minute topographic map.

Miles and Directions

0.0 Trailhead on eastern side of parking area loop.
1.0 Trap Spring.
2.0 Mule Ears Spring and rock-walled corral.
3.0 Escarpment overlooking Smoky Creek.
3.5 Junction with Smoky Creek Trail.

Mule Ears Peaks

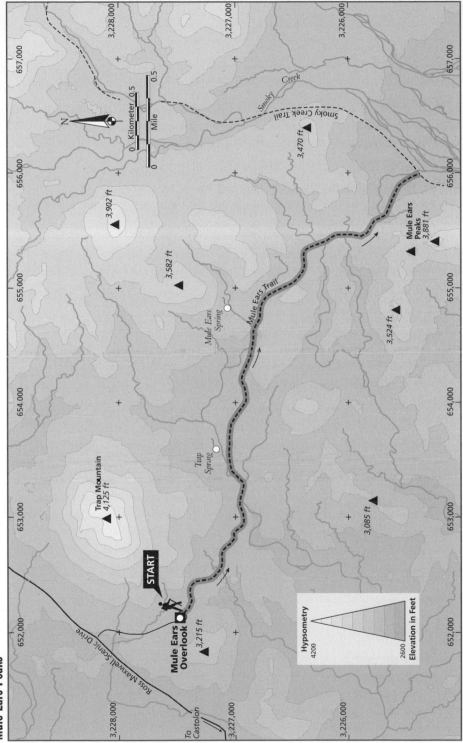

19 Smoky Creek

General description: A backpack through desert foothills on the southwest side of the Chisos Mountains that is often done in sections.
Distance: 15.3 miles one way.
Approximate hiking time: 7.5 to 8 hours.
Difficulty: Strenuous, if done in its entirety.

Traffic: Light.
Trail surface: Dirt path and sand, gravel, and cobbles of dry desert wash.
Topo maps: Smoky Creek (southern section), Cerro Castellan (central section), Emory Peak (northern section).

Finding the trailhead: The Smoky Creek Trail complex can be reached from several points. On the northern end, it intersects with the Dodson Trail about 3 miles east of Homer Wilson Blue Creek Ranch.

The central section of Smoky Creek is reached via the Mule Ears Trail, which begins at the Mule Ears Viewpoint parking area. The Mule Ears Trail descends into the Smoky Creek drainage about 1.5 miles east of Mule Ears Spring, making a total hike of 3.5 miles from the Mule Ears trailhead to Smoky Creek.

The southern end of the Smoky Creek drainage crosses the rugged River Road West, midway between Buenos Aires and Black Dike primitive campsites. Check your topographic map to find this point. Both the road and the creek cut through a low ridge known as the Sierra de Chino at the same point. Inquire about road conditions on the primitive, unpaved River Road, which often requires four-wheel drive, before attempting to drive it.

The Hike

Varied topography, numerous springs and seeps, interesting canyons, and an endless sky make the Smoky Creek area popular with experienced backpackers during the cooler months. In spite of the heavy use that some parts of the drainage receive during college spring break and the Thanksgiving holiday, it is easy to find plenty of solitude most of the year. The primitive nature and remoteness of Smoky Creek provide rewarding challenges to experienced hikers, but require map-reading skills, plenty of water, knowledge of desert travel, and good judgment.

It is not necessary to hike the entire Smoky Creek Trail; it offers many options for long or short hikes in the middle and lower Chihuahuan Desert. Water can sometimes be surprisingly abundant at numerous springs along the way. However, hikers should not assume it will be available without first checking with park rangers. If water is available, Smoky Creek can be a particularly attractive hiking area except during the hottest months.

For the most part, the route follows the dry wash drainage of its namesake, but it occasionally leaves the drainage to bypass pour-offs or difficult areas. Good map-reading and route-finding skills are essential to navigate the many confluences of dry washes, especially when hiking north, or upstream. Much of this hike is in the loose gravel of the Smoky Creek wash, where there is no distinct trail.

A small stream trickles over a low waterfall on the Smoky Creek Trail. PHOTO: MARY K. MANNING

Smoky Creek

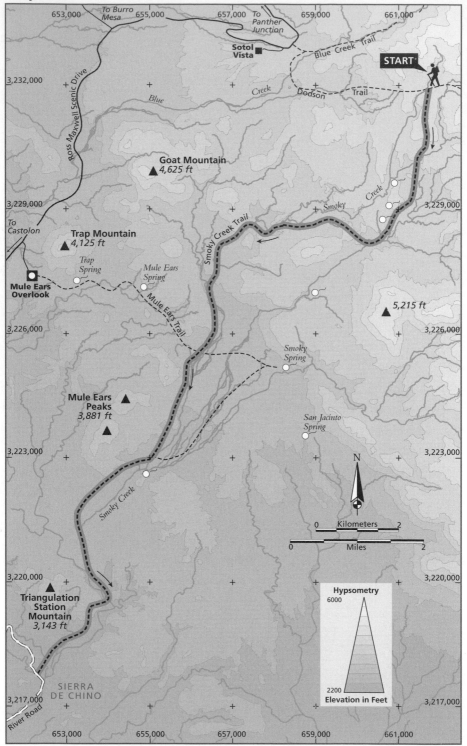

Several infrequently traveled trails and routes intersect the Smoky Creek drainage, giving adventurous hikers plenty of opportunity to explore. Always remember to climb out of the wash before setting up your camp; this drainage floods regularly during the rainy season.

Hikers traveling north to south, downstream, usually do not have much problem following the route, because tributary drainages flow into Smoky Creek, helping to guide you toward the main Smoky Creek drainage. However, south-to-north travelers can easily become confused at the numerous tributary confluences, where a decision to follow the wrong branch can lead unwary hikers astray. Even properly backtracking a route that was walked earlier can be a challenge. For this reason, it is critically important to have the pertinent 7.5-minute topographic maps and to constantly keep track of your position on them.

The northern end of the Smoky Creek route intersects the Dodson Trail hike about 3 miles east of the Homer Wilson Blue Creek Ranch. Hikers exiting Smoky Creek at this point must remain alert to find the Dodson Trail. A large rock cairn on the northwestern creek bank marks the trail, but many hikers miss it.

Be sure to remain alert for rock cairns in the northern half of the Smoky Creek route. Impassable or difficult sections of the main drainage are bypassed by segments of trail that shortcut parts of the drainage or parallel the creek on the slopes high above the wash. Some of these trail sections are marked on the topographic maps; others are revealed only to the vigilant hiker.

Be sure to note one important difference between the marked route on the Emory Peak 7.5-minute topographic map and the current route of the trail. About 3 miles south of the Dodson Trail junction, the current trail exits a wash and proceeds northwest across a pass to re-enter the main Smoky Creek drainage. This pass may be found about 3.5 inches from the western edge of the Emory Peak map, north of the trail and between two low peaks marked on the map as "4026" and "4065." A sharp bend in the drainage marks the exit point on the map, and a high cut bank on the northwestern bank serves as a landmark to hikers. If floods have not washed it away, a metal sign indicates the proper direction to the pass. North of the pass, the route re-enters the Smoky Creek drainage directly east of Peak 4065 and proceeds downstream. The current route rejoins the marked route near the eastern edge of the Cerro Castellan topographic map.

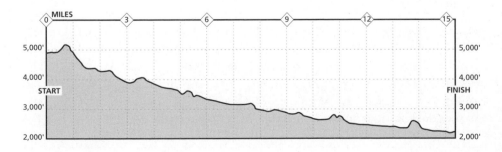

To explore the central section of the drainage, hike east from Mule Ears Spring about 1.5 miles. The trail skirts the Mule Ears Peaks on the north side before joining the Smoky Creek route in the drainage. By leaving the creek at this point and hiking about 1 mile east cross-country and slightly south across the broad drainage valley (check your topographic map), it's possible to make an excursion to Smoky Spring. The remains of a stone-walled structure and corral are just above the spring to the east. Explore some of the other side canyons in this area, too, if you have time; many of them harbor small seeps that support vegetation and wildlife.

From this point south, the Smoky Creek route remains almost constantly in the wash and is relatively easy to follow if you are hiking south. Cairns may or may not mark the route. While the drainage is very wide in most places, with extensive views, the creekbed narrows occasionally, creating short but impressive canyons. About 1 mile from River Road West, you'll skirt the eastern flank of Triangulation Station Mountain, named for its usefulness as a landmark to surveyors.

Miles and Directions

0.0 Dodson Trail junction.

8.5 Mule Ears Trail junction.

15.3 River Road trailhead.

20 Homer Wilson Blue Creek Ranch

General description: A day hike to a historic ranch on the southwestern slopes of the Chisos Mountains.
Distance: 0.25 mile one way.
Approximate hiking time: 15 minutes.

Difficulty: Easy.
Traffic: Heavy.
Trail surface: Dirt path.
Topo map: Emory Peak.

Finding the trailhead: From the Santa Elena Junction, about 13 miles west of Panther Junction on the road to Study Butte and Alpine, drive south on the Ross Maxwell Scenic Drive toward Castolon and Santa Elena Canyon. The trailhead lies at the paved pullout on the left at 8.1 miles.

The Hike

Homer Wilson Blue Creek Ranch was the heart of Homer Wilson's ranching operations in the Chisos Mountains before the park was established in the 1940s. The house was a line camp lived in for many years by Wilson's foreman, Lott Felts. The house lies in the bottom of Blue Creek Canyon, a major drainage on the southwestern side of the Chisos Mountains. The house can be seen from above, from the start of the trail right by the parking lot.

Homer Wilson Blue Creek Ranch

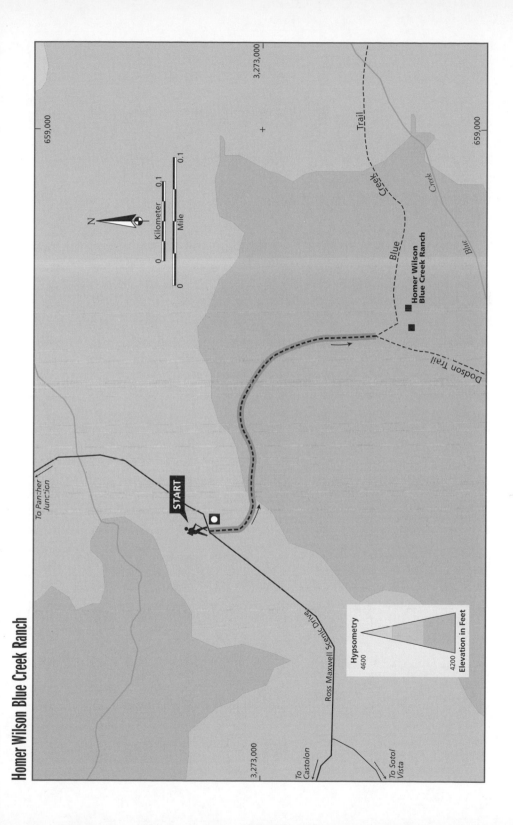

Homer Wilson's line camp still stands in the bottom of Blue Creek Canyon.

The well-used trail descends into the canyon on an old road with a short, moderate grade. It then crosses the relatively flat canyon bottom to the house. The native stone structure is in relatively good repair, although the window glass is missing. Thick walls, a flagstone floor, a big fireplace, and a wood viga-and-cane ceiling give a solid, homey feel to the house. In the back is a large, pleasant roofed porch. A storeroom, ruins of a bunkhouse, corral, dipping vat, chicken coop, and other ranching facilities adjoin the house. To obtain water for livestock, a pipeline was run several miles up the canyon to a spring. Domestic water was obtained from a cistern built on the hill by the parking lot.

The short trail to the ranch house is also a starting point for two major park trails, the Blue Creek Trail and the Dodson Trail. The Blue Creek Trail climbs Blue Creek Canyon into the high Chisos Mountains and joins the Laguna Meadow Trail. The Dodson Trail cuts across the southern, lower part of the mountains to the Juniper Canyon Road.

Miles and Directions

0.0 Homer Wilson Blue Creek Ranch parking area.
0.25 Homer Wilson Blue Creek Ranch.

21 Tuff Canyon

General description: A day hike into a narrow canyon carved out of soft volcanic tuff, plus several overlooks.

Distance: 0.4 mile one way.

Approximate hiking time: 30 minutes.

Difficulty: Easy.

Traffic: Heavy.

Trail surface: Dirt path.

Topo map: Cerro Castellan.

Finding the trailhead: From Santa Elena Junction, about 13 miles west of Panther Junction on the road to Study Butte and Alpine, drive south on the Ross Maxwell Scenic Drive toward Castolon and Santa Elena Canyon. The trailhead lies at the large paved pullout on the right after 19.9 miles.

Water has carved a narrow canyon through soft volcanic tuff.

Tuff Canyon

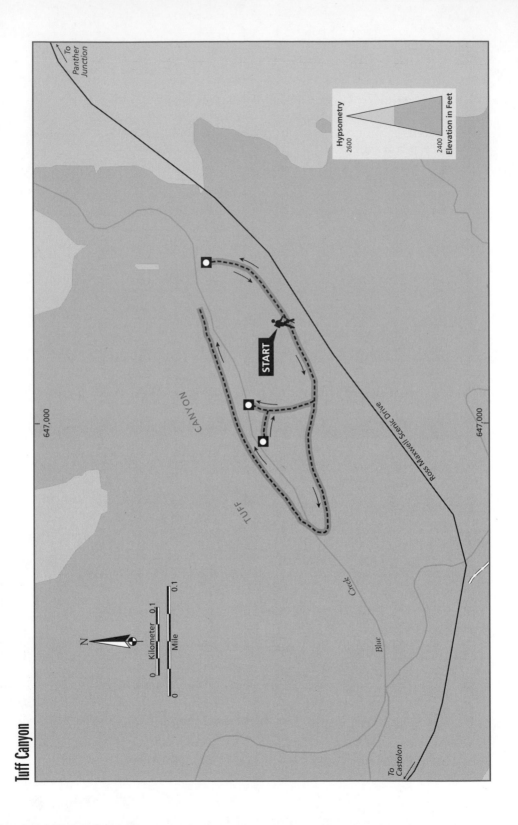

The Hike

Tuff Canyon is a small, narrow, sheer-walled canyon carved into a layer of light gray tuff by Blue Creek, one of the largest drainages of the Chisos Mountains. The tuff was created during an explosive volcanic eruption that blew the molten rock into small particles, or ash. As this hot, glowing ash settled back to the ground, heat and the pressure of overlying layers hardened the ash into a soft rock called tuff. Water easily eroded this tuff into a canyon along Blue Creek.

Start the hike with the canyon overlooks. From the uphill, northeast side of the parking pullout, take a very short trail to a good overlook of the upper end of Tuff Canyon. From the downhill, southwest side of the parking pullout, a second trail heads toward the canyon. A short side trail quickly splits off to the right and leads to two more good overlooks. Be sure to stay on the trails to the overlooks where there are protective handrails. The tuff on the canyon rim is soft and crumbly, making a serious fall easy. Hikers may be below, so don't throw rocks or other objects into the canyon.

After returning to the fork on the second trail, turn right and follow the main trail downhill a short distance to the wash at the canyon mouth. Follow the wash upstream into the canyon. Except when the sun is high overhead, much of the bottom lies in cool shade thrown by the high, close-set walls. Bees are sometimes active in a hive tucked up high in one canyon wall. Farther up the canyon, near the trail's end, hard, erosion-resistant layers of lava create ledges in the bottom.

Return to the trailhead via the same route. The soft, crumbly rock makes taking shortcuts up out of the canyon hazardous, plus creates unsightly erosion scars.

The dry creek can be followed many miles upstream, although Tuff Canyon ends relatively soon. Blue Creek eventually crosses the Ross Maxwell Scenic Drive, passes beneath Sotol Vista, and climbs high into the Chisos Mountains. There is no formal trail, however, so hikers should be prepared for rough cross-country travel.

Miles and Directions

0.0 Tuff Canyon parking lot.

0.2 Bottom of canyon.

0.4 End of trail in canyon bottom.

Minor additional mileage comes from short overlook trails.

22 Santa Elena Canyon

General description: A day hike into a spectacular canyon cut by the Rio Grande.

Distance: 0.8 mile one way.

Approximate hiking time: 30 to 45 minutes.

Difficulty: Easy.

Traffic: Heavy.

Trail surface: Dirt and paved path.

Topo map: Castolon.

Finding the trailhead: The trail begins at the Santa Elena Canyon parking area at the end of the Ross Maxwell Scenic Drive, about 42 miles southwest of Panther Junction.

The Hike

This hike takes you into the mouth of one of the three major canyons of the Rio Grande in Big Bend National Park. Because the 1,500-foot-deep canyon is spectacular and the hike is easy, this trail is one of the most popular in the park. Summer temperatures frequently exceed 100 degrees Fahrenheit, so hike early in the morning from about April through October and carry water. Fortunately, there is shade in the canyon. Although there is little net elevation change in the hike, the trail does require a short 80-foot climb up the canyon wall and back down to river level.

From the parking area, the trail runs through a stand of giant river cane and tamarisk before dropping into the Terlingua Creek drainage. The creek may be completely dry or flowing strongly. Use caution and common sense in deciding whether to cross if the water is deep and muddy. Once you cross Terlingua Creek, you immediately climb a fairly steep, paved trail. Rest as needed as you climb and enjoy the views behind you. To the east and southeast the floodplain of the Rio Grande and the ribbon of river wind through the desert; to the northeast rise the Sierra Quemada and Chisos Mountains.

The cliff on your right as you approach the canyon is the most easterly edge of the Mesa de Anguila, a large mesa in the dry western portion of Big Bend National Park. To your left across the Rio Grande rises the impressive Sierra Ponce, the northern boundary of Mexico and the other canyon wall.

As you reach the trail's high point, you get your first good view of the river in the canyon. From here you descend a series of steep log steps to the narrow river floodplain. The trail follows the river through thick, shady stands of mesquite, cane, and tamarisk, eventually passing under a huge, angular boulder. Just past the boulder the trail winds its way to the wet sand at the river's edge. Several trails twist through the boulders that litter the narrow floodplain, but eventually the river cuts off the path at a sheer canyon wall, blocking further access upstream.

Santa Elena Canyon is the most popular float trip
at Big Bend National Park. ▶

Santa Elena Canyon

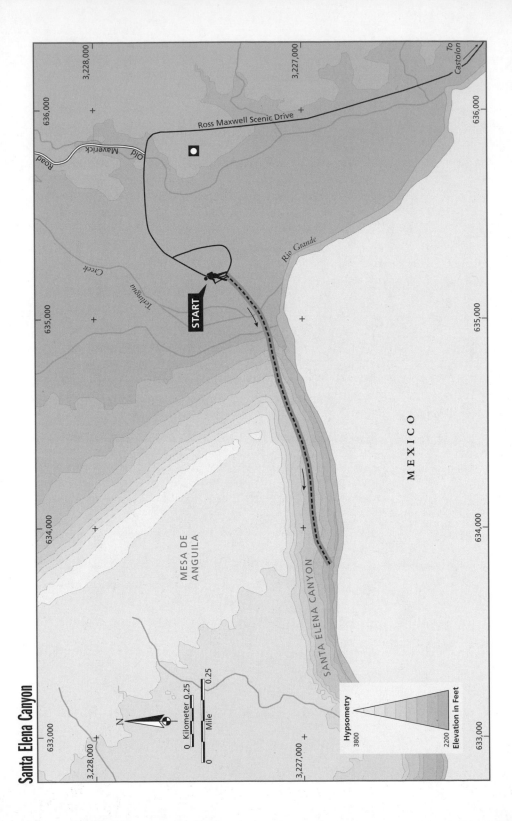

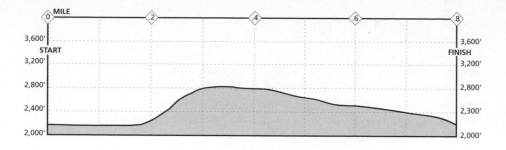

Of the three major canyons of the Rio Grande in Big Bend National Park, Santa Elena Canyon is the most frequently boated. Fifteen-hundred-foot walls tower over the river, creating a narrow gorge into which the sun shines for only a short time each day. Although most of the river is fairly flat, the Rockslide, a class IV/V rapid, adds excitement and challenge to the trip for the thousands of people who float the canyon each year. Although most boaters travel through the canyon on guided trips arranged by outfitters, it is possible for experienced boaters to float Santa Elena Canyon using their own equipment and skills. However, this is not a trip for novice boaters. Be sure to inquire at any park visitor center for more information and permits. Low water levels caused by excessive Mexican water withdrawals and drought often make float trips difficult.

Miles and Directions

0.0 Trailhead at Santa Elena Canyon parking area.

0.8 End of trail, where river cuts off the riverbank.

23 Dominguez Spring

General description: A day hike or backpacking trip through the Chihuahuan Desert to the Dominguez historic site.
Distance: 7 miles one way.
Approximate hiking time: 3.5 to 4 hours.

Difficulty: Difficult.
Traffic: Very light.
Trail surface: Dirt path.
Topo maps: Reed Camp and Emory Peak.

Finding the trailhead: The Dominguez Spring trailhead is located 23 miles from the west end of River Road and is well-marked with a sign. The west end of River Road begins from the Ross Maxwell Scenic Drive near Castolon. River Road is often rough and passable only by high-clearance and/or four-wheel-drive vehicles. Be sure to inquire about road conditions before beginning this trip. Vehicle break-ins sometimes occur at the trailhead.

The Hike

The Dominguez Spring Trail can be a strenuous day hike, but is better done as a backpacking trip. Although water is sometimes available at the spring, it is unreliable. Hikers should plan to carry all their water. This trail should be considered a cool season hike, since daytime temperatures of more than 100 degrees Fahrenheit are common during summer. In spite of the challenges of this trail, those who persevere are rewarded with beautiful scenery and an intriguing historic site.

The first 4.5 miles of the trail follow the route of an old road that heads toward the southern end of the Chisos Mountains. It crosses open, gently sloping desert country as it travels north from River Road. As you hike up the gradually ascending trail, you have beautiful views of Dominguez Mountain, the singular cone-shaped mountain ahead and slightly to your right. This mountain was named for Félix Dominguez, whose cattle grazed in this part of the Big Bend in the 1890s.

After the first 2 miles, you will notice a dense population of a cactus called blind prickly pear. Like the other species of prickly pear cacti at Big Bend, it bears a flattened, pear-shaped pad from which comes its common name. However, unlike other prickly pear species, it appears to have no spines, only small tufts of a fuzzy material dotting the pads. In reality, these seemingly benign tufts are clusters of very tiny spines that fall off of the cacti pads with the slightest disturbance. The name blind prickly pear may have come about during droughts when livestock would sometimes eat the cacti pads. As the animals bit into the pads, the story goes, the tiny spines would fly off into the air and, sometimes, into their eyes, resulting in blindness. During periods of drought, stockmen such as Dominguez would sometimes burn the spines off the different prickly pears to feed their livestock.

After the first 4.5 miles, the old road disappears into a wash as beautiful views of the canyons of the southern Chisos Mountains become apparent. Rock cairns continue to mark the trail as they did along the old road. In another mile, the trail

Dominguez Spring

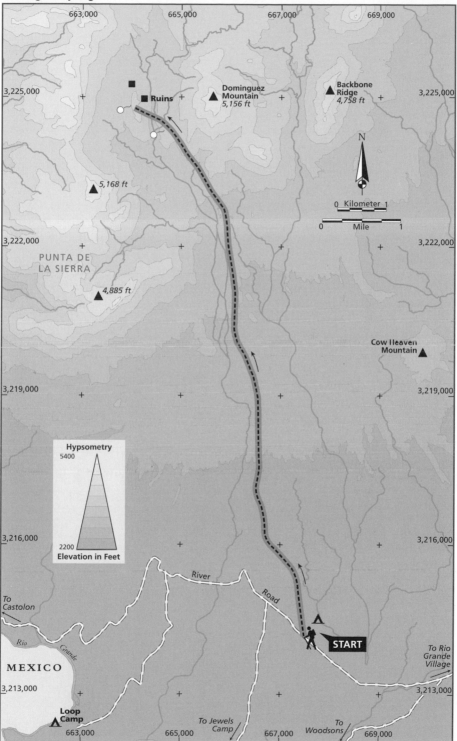

663,000   665,000   667,000   669,000

3,225,000

■
■ **Ruins**

▲ **Dominguez Mountain** *5,156 ft*

▲ **Backbone Ridge** *4,758 ft*

N

0   Kilometer   1
0   Mile   1

▲ *5,168 ft*

3,222,000

PUNTA DE LA SIERRA

▲ *4,885 ft*

Cow Heaven Mountain ▲

3,219,000

Hypsometry

5400

2200
Elevation in Feet

3,216,000

River

Road

START

To Castolon

Rio Grande

MEXICO

3,213,000

▲ **Loop Camp**

To Jewels Camp

To Woodsons

To Rio Grande Village

663,000   665,000   667,000   669,000

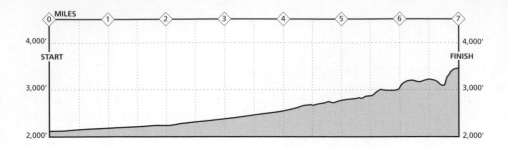

reaches the remnants of an old ranch fence. After the final 1.5 miles, a rock cairn in the shape of an arrow directs hikers to a side wash on the left that leads to the historic site. Floods or other events could wipe out this marker, so be sure to check your map regularly. The ruins of several corrals, two rock houses, and the ruins of a dam in the wash are some of the developments left behind by the Fisk family. They lived here into the late 1930s, when their land became part of the new national park.

Take all the photos and memories that you want, but please leave all remnants of the settlement at this site undisturbed so that others may enjoy them; also, they are protected by federal law.

Miles and Directions

0.0 Dominguez Spring trailhead on River Road.

4.5 Trail leaves route of old road.

5.5 Old ranch fence.

7.0 End of trail at ruins of old ranch settlement.

24 Elephant Tusk

General description: A backpack on a lightly traveled route through ridges and rocky drainages in the Chisos Mountains foothills.
Distance: 8 miles one way.
Approximate hiking time: 4 hours.

Difficulty: Strenuous.
Traffic: Very light.
Trail surface: Dirt path.
Topo maps: Emory Peak and Glenn Spring.

Finding the trailhead: Reaching just the start of the Elephant Tusk Trail requires dedication and preparation. The northern end of the route joins the Dodson Trail below the South Rim. Marked with a sign, the junction is about a 5-mile walk along the Dodson Trail from either the Homer Wilson Blue Creek Ranch or Juniper Canyon trailhead. The marked Homer Wilson Blue Creek Ranch trailhead is about 8.1 miles south along the Ross Maxwell Scenic Drive from its junction with the Panther Junction-Study Butte highway. Reaching the Juniper Canyon trailhead requires a 14-mile drive along the rough Glenn Spring and Juniper Canyon backcountry roads. The trailhead lies at the end of Juniper Canyon Road. Either end of the Dodson Trail may also be reached by hiking from the Basin via the Outer Mountain Loop.

The trail's southern end is at the Elephant Tusk primitive campsite near Talley Mountain on Black Gap Road. It may be reached via River Road or Glenn Spring Road. Black Gap Road is notoriously rough; consider this access only if you have a high-clearance, four-wheel-drive vehicle. The road's southern end is usually in better condition and offers easier trailhead access. Be sure to check with park rangers for road conditions before attempting this route.

The Hike

A hike could hardly begin in a more dramatic setting. At the Dodson/Elephant Tusk Trail junction, the massive cliffs of the South Rim climb nearly 2,500 feet above you. To the north is the volcanic ridgeline of Crown Mountain, while to the south are the wild canyons and heights of the Sierra Quemada. In the far distance the mountains and desert valleys of Mexico continue to the horizon.

Near the beginning of the trail you can see the canyons and ridges you will cross. Pause for a moment to locate obvious landmarks. Consult your map often and use it to follow your progress if you are unfamiliar with the area. Water from springs is sometimes available within the Fresno Creek and Elephant Tusk drainages, but you should check with a ranger before depending on these water sources.

After leaving the Dodson route, the trail winds its way down near the rim of the Fresno drainage. Notice the excellent example of a volcanic dike that crosses the canyon and continues beyond the trail. There are a few very nice campsites in this area. Farther down, the route turns east into a side drainage that soon joins Fresno Creek near the base of Tortuga Mountain. Water is usually available from a spring at this location. The trail continues down the creekbed, then turns west up the next

The Elephant Tusk Trail follows several drainages near the base of pointed Elephant Tusk.

large wash and continues in it for about 200 yards. Look for rock cairns marking the spot where the trail begins to climb across the ridge to the Elephant Tusk drainage.

As the trail enters the Elephant Tusk drainage, it turns downstream to meander its way around the side of Elephant Tusk Peak. The mountain is formed by igneous rock, which is impervious to water, forcing the water to remain at or very near the surface. For this reason, the area contains several usually reliable springs. There are scattered stands of moisture-loving plants such as cattails, willows, and cottonwood trees. Look closely for clumps of mosses and leathery ferns. Virtually all the trees have been damaged by flood-driven boulders, so don't camp in any wash bottom in the area.

Watch carefully to locate the trail as it climbs out of the northeast side of the drainage below Elephant Tusk; it is hard to follow until the bank flattens out farther downstream. If you lose the trail, you may simply continue down the wash until it widens, then climb out to rejoin the trail. If you follow the wash, you will come to an enormous boulder lodged between the walls of the canyon. The boulder blocks the way, so you will have to slide down a small pour-off into a shallow pool of water.

After leaving the wash, the trail crosses some low hills to the southeast, then turns south into an arroyo. There are some excellent campsites in the area. The remainder of the route follows the arroyo across open desert to the Elephant Tusk campsite on the Black Gap Road near the base of Talley Mountain.

Elephant Tusk

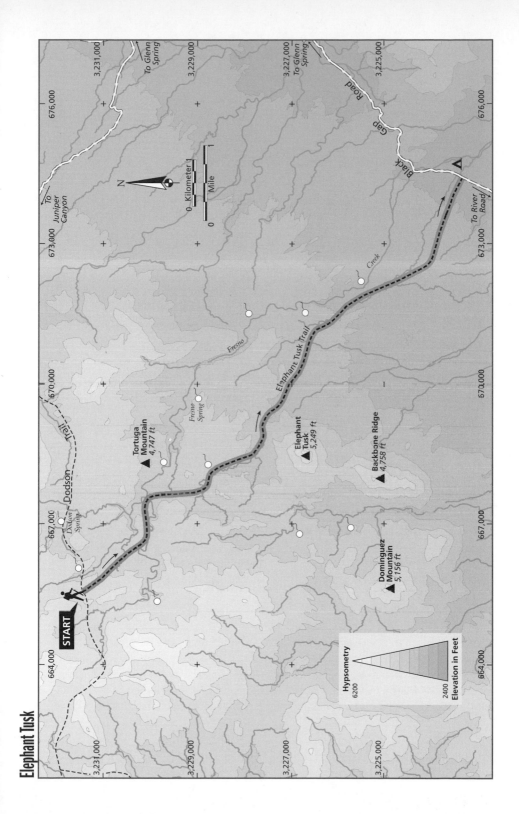

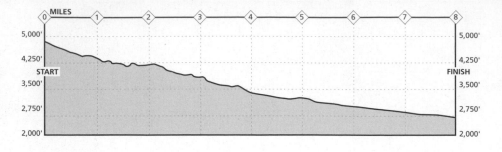

Miles and Directions

0.0 Trailhead at junction with Dodson Trail. The trail turns south toward the top of the ridge.

0.8 Trail drops into a small wash, then joins Fresno Creek drainage near the base of Tortuga Mountain.

1.9 Trail leaves Fresno Creek drainage and turns up another wash for about 200 yards before climbing out of the wash to the west and crossing the ridgeline.

2.8 Trail enters the Elephant Tusk drainage, where it remains for the next 1.6 miles.

4.4 Trail exits the drainage on the left side, then turns across some low hills toward the southeast.

6.1 Trail descends into a wide desert arroyo, then climbs out and parallels it.

8.0 Elephant Tusk primitive campsite on the Black Gap Road.

25 Mariscal Canyon Rim

General description: A steep day hike to the rim of spectacular Mariscal Canyon, one of three major Rio Grande canyons in Big Bend National Park.
Distance: 3.3 miles one way.
Approximate hiking time: 1.5 to 2 hours.
Difficulty: Strenuous.

Traffic: Light.
Trail surface: Dirt path.
Topo map: Mariscal Mountain. This map does not show the Mariscal Rim Trail. The Trails Illustrated map shows the trail, but not accurately on Mariscal Mountain.

Finding the trailhead: From the road to Rio Grande Village, turn right onto River Road about 15 miles from Panther Junction. Follow River Road about 23 miles to the side road to Talley on the left. From the Castolon area, take River Road from the west about 28 miles to the Talley junction. Both backcountry routes usually require a high-clearance vehicle and sometimes four-wheel drive. The western part of River Road is usually rougher. Follow Talley Road for about 6 miles. About 0.5 mile past Talley Campsite 2 on your right and about 0.5 mile from the end of

Sheer cliffs drop more than 1,000 feet from the ▶
Mariscal Canyon Rim to the Rio Grande.

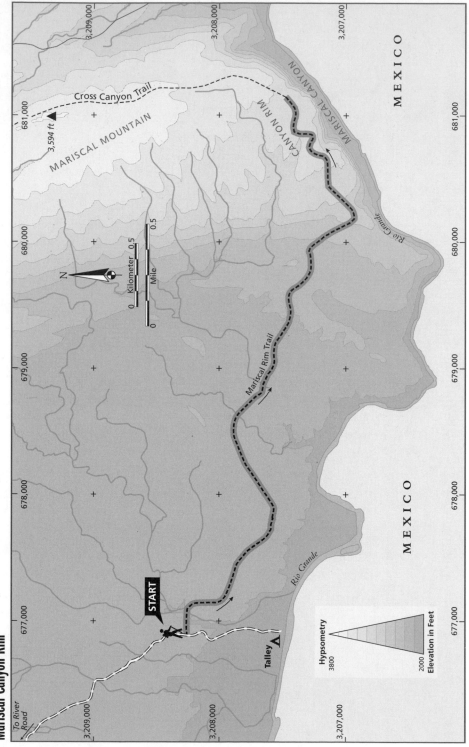

Mariscal Canyon Rim

the road at the river is the parking area for the Mariscal Canyon Rim trailhead on your left. Be sure to inquire with park rangers about road conditions before making this trip.

Unfortunately, some parking areas along the river, including this one, are frequented by thieves. The vehicles themselves are usually safe, but do not leave valuables (or, ideally, anything) inside them.

The Hike

The geography of Big Bend National Park offers hikes to the river, into canyons, through badlands, or up mountains. But nowhere in Big Bend can you experience such a magnificent blending of landscapes into one trip as you can by hiking to the rim of Mariscal Canyon. This hike combines rugged landscapes, distant panoramas, and wilderness solitude all in one.

From February through June this trail is closed to hiking because of peregrine falcons nesting along the canyon rim. Check at a ranger station for specific closure dates.

Avoid hiking this route during the hot months of the year, often from as early as April to as late as October. There is no water or shade, and afternoon temperatures frequently exceed 100 degrees Fahrenheit. Also, use care near the sheer cliffs of the canyon rim at the end of the trail. The canyon walls drop 1,200 feet straight down to the river from the rim.

The first 1.5 miles are flat and easy. The second part of the hike begins climbing moderately, but steepens into a strenuous ascent up the side of Mariscal Mountain.

The most confusing portion of this hike will be the first 300 yards from the trailhead. Your immediate destination is the small hill just to the east of the parking area. Between you and the hill, however, is a mesquite-lined drainage with no established trail. Simply work your way down into the wash through the thorny brush and up the other side of this small drainage. Once you have crossed this slight obstacle, look around the small hill in the direction of the river for the trail. It is well marked with rock cairns.

The easy first 1.5 miles of this hike parallel the river on a bench above the floodplain. The route travels across colorful shales and siltstones of the Pen Formation, which are penetrated by various intrusions of darker igneous rocks. In their geologic past, some of the sedimentary layers were "baked" by the igneous activity, adding to their color. Crystalline veins streak through the fractured rocks, and unique nodules

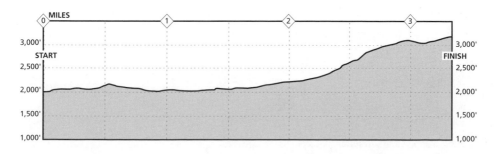

and concretions litter the area. Even the rock cairns marking the first 1 mile of this route contain a mixture of rocks that mirror the geologic diversity of this area.

The sparse vegetation along this part of the route helps make travel here easy. Apparently the shales, marls, mudstones, and other rocks of the Pen Formation, combined with low precipitation levels, provide a poor environment for plant growth. Here, the desert contains only spotty examples of ocotillo, prickly pear, creosote, stunted whitethorn acacia, and Mexican rubber plant or guayule.

After the first 1.5 miles, the trail enters and follows a dry wash. It is along this stretch that the Pen Formation gives way to thin-bedded, chalky gray limestones and shales of the Boquillas Formation. After leaving the drainage, the trail begins a moderately strenuous climb toward cliffs along the ridge of Mariscal Mountain and the canyon itself.

As the trail climbs higher, many cacti become evident, including Texas rainbow, eagle's claw, and pincushion varieties. One cactus, the silverspine cane cholla, is a variety of cane cholla endemic to the dry slopes of Mariscal Mountain and grows naturally nowhere else on Earth.

As you climb, look west; the meandering floodplain of the Rio Grande looks like a narrow green oasis sprawling across the vast Chihuahuan Desert landscape. To the north, the eroded geologic layers alongside Mariscal Mountain's anticlinal fold have created an impressive series of hogbacks. The uppermost of these scalloped-looking ridges, closest to the massive limestone walls of Mariscal Mountain, is capped by the Del Rio Clay Formation.

At the base of the cliffs the trail momentarily levels off. If you are backpacking, this level terrace makes for a pleasant campsite. From here, the trail cuts sharply to the left and switchbacks up to the top of Mariscal Mountain. The next 0.25 mile is the most strenuous part of the hike; it gains another 400 feet as it switchbacks through the massive Santa Elena limestone cliffs of Mariscal Mountain. Once on top, however, the trail levels off and generally parallels the canyon several hundred yards back from the rim. At almost any point once the trail levels off, select your own route and work your way over to the precipitous rim. The vertigo-inducing overlooks are magnificent.

To return, retrace your route back to the trailhead. For some individuals, continuing on to Cross Canyon and to the Cross Canyon Trail may be an option. The trip is recommended, however, for only the most experienced hikers and backpackers. The old pack trail from the rim to Cross Canyon is poorly defined and has no water. The descent into Cross Canyon is rough. Once you locate the Cross Canyon Trail, the climb back up and over the eastern half of Mariscal Mountain to Solis is quite strenuous.

Miles and Directions

0.0 Mariscal Canyon Rim trailhead at Talley.

1.5 Trail begins to climb from flats above river.

3.3 Mariscal Canyon Rim.

26 Cross Canyon

General description: A backpack or strenuous day hike up Mariscal Mountain to the Mariscal Rim Trail, or along the mountain then down to the Rio Grande in Mariscal Canyon.

Distance: 7 miles one way.

Approximate hiking time: 3.5 hours.

Difficulty: Strenuous and very difficult to follow.

Traffic: Very light.

Trail surface: Dirt path and cross country.

Topo maps: Solis and Mariscal Mountain. The trail is not marked on the USGS topographic maps. It is partly marked on the Trails Illustrated map, but this map is not adequate by itself.

Finding the trailhead: The Cross Canyon Trail begins at Solis primitive campsite 3, reached via River Road. The turnoff to Solis lies on the left about 14 miles from the Rio Grande Village road along River Road. High-clearance and/or four-wheel-drive vehicles are usually required; check on road conditions before beginning the drive. Be sure to ask about security conditions before parking at Solis; theft from unattended vehicles is sometimes a problem. Do not leave valuables (or, ideally, anything) in your vehicle. Be careful not to get stuck in the sandy parking area.

The Hike

Rarely hiked and difficult to follow, the Cross Canyon Trail is for strong, experienced hikers only. Loose, rocky footing and an indistinct path require patience and good map-reading skills. Tremendous vistas and access to the Rio Grande reward those hikers who make the extra effort necessary to follow the route. The 7-mile, one-way distance shown above is from the trailhead to the river on the left fork of the trail. The distance from the trailhead to the Mariscal Rim Trail is similar.

The trail can be indistinct, and discernible in many areas only by the fairly frequent rock cairns. Some cairns are impressively large, while others are small and easy to miss. The trail is not marked on the topographic maps; it is essential that you follow the cairn-marked route. You must be prepared for very rough, nearly cross-country hiking conditions. The trail is marked on a reference map at the Panther Junction Visitor Center; it is a good idea to copy the route onto your map before you go.

After it leaves Solis, the trail briefly parallels a wash, then begins a gentle climb toward the shoulder of Mariscal Mountain. About a mile from the trailhead, the land begins to rise more steeply as you hike beside a small desert canyon. At the head of the canyon, at roughly 3.3 miles, the trail turns south and skirts the base of a ridge for about a mile before climbing again to a small pass where the trail to the rim of Mariscal Canyon splits to the west, while the Cross Canyon Trail begins to descend to the south. Finding this pass is crucial. The junction is marked with a broad, low cairn and a rock "Y" laid on the ground at its foot. From here, you have a sweeping view of the Maderas del Carmen and Sierra del Carmen in Mexico, Chilicotal

Boaters float through Mariscal Canyon just below Cross Canyon.

Mountain in the relative foreground to the east, the Dead Horse Mountains to the northeast on the horizon, and the Chisos Mountains to the north.

If you go right at this fork, the trail winds up a small drainage to a saddle, contours around along the edge of another drainage back to the northwest, and then climbs and follows a high ridge south to the rim of Mariscal Canyon. Here it joins the Mariscal Rim Trail. The views along this ridge are spectacular. You can see Cerro Castellan, Santa Elena Canyon, all of the Chisos Mountains, and dramatic views of Mexico.

Alternatively, the left branch leads down a steep canyon into Cross Canyon. At the beginning of the descent, part of the southern wall of Mariscal Canyon is clearly visible. Again, following the cairns is critical as you descend toward the Rio Grande. The trail leads along the side of one canyon before it crosses a saddle and drops into another canyon on the right. The trail keeps heading toward the river as it crosses a few small washes and then follows a ridge along a deepening canyon. It drops steeply toward the river, providing good views of the river and the canyon mouth. When you finally reach the bedrock floor of Cross Canyon, you must cross it and climb the

Cross Canyon

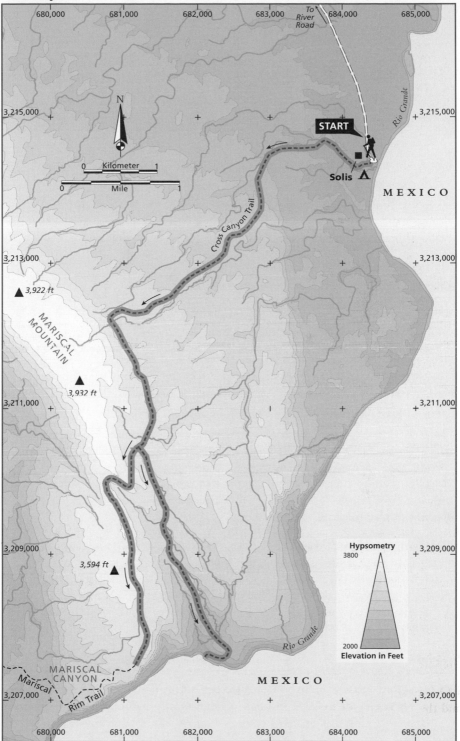

MEXICO

Rio Grande

START

Solis

Cross Canyon Trail

N

Kilometer
0   1

Mile
0   1

3,215,000

3,213,000

▲ 3,922 ft

MARISCAL MOUNTAIN

▲ 3,932 ft

3,211,000

3,594 ft ▲

Rio Grande

MEXICO

MARISCAL CANYON

Mariscal
Rim Trail

3,209,000

3,207,000

To
River
Road

Hypsometry
3800

2000
Elevation in Feet

680,000   681,000   682,000   683,000   684,000   685,000

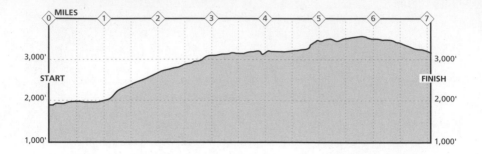

hill before you, hiking above and behind two rock outcrops. It is tempting to follow the canyon floor downstream, but this will lead you to the top of an impassable pour-off more than 50 feet high, from where you can see your destination—the Rio Grande—without being able to reach it. Past the rock outcrops, the trail traverses a ridge and then heads west toward the Cross Canyon drainage and ends at the river.

Miles and Directions

0.0 Trailhead at Solis.

4.5 Trail fork at small pass. Go right to the Mariscal Rim Trail, left to the river.

7.0 Rio Grande in Cross Canyon.

27 Hot Springs

General description: A day hike past historic buildings and a large hot spring on the banks of the Rio Grande.
Distance: 1 mile loop.
Approximate hiking time: 30 minutes.

Difficulty: Easy.
Traffic: Heavy.
Trail surface: Dirt path.
Topo map: Boquillas.

Finding the trailhead: From park headquarters at Panther Junction, drive a little more than 17 miles along the Rio Grande Village highway to the marked Hot Springs turnoff on the right. Follow the maintained dirt road 1.7 miles to the parking lot at its end. The last 0.5 mile or so of the road is very narrow and winding and is impassable to RVs, trailers, or very wide vehicles. Drivers of such vehicles will need to park in a parking area on the right side of the road before the narrow, one-way section of road begins.

The Hike

J. O. Langford and his family homesteaded here at the confluence of Tornillo Creek and the Rio Grande in 1909 and built a small health spa using hot spring waters.

J. O. Langford's general store and post office still stands at Hot Springs.

He also hoped to regain his health after suffering from malaria growing up in Mississippi. With the help of a stonemason, he built a large stone bathhouse over the main hot spring. In 1913, unrest and civil war in Mexico caused the Langfords to leave the border area. In 1927, they returned and built a combined post office, trading post, and motel for guests. The Langfords finally left permanently in 1942 after selling their land to the government for inclusion in the new national park. Maggy Smith operated the resort for several more years as a park concession before it finally closed for good.

The ruins of the Livingston house adjoin the trailhead parking lot. Within a few yards, the trail passes the relatively intact post office, shaded by a non-native palm. A short distance beyond the post office on the trail lie the former motel units, with murals painted on the interior walls. A clump of more exotic palms shades the sandy riverbank above the confluence of Tornillo Creek and the river.

Be sure to look closely for painted pictographs on the cliff walls just past the motel units. Various Indian groups lived in and traveled through the area long before the Langfords and other settlers arrived. The trail passes through a short, shady

Hot Springs; Hot Springs Canyon Rim

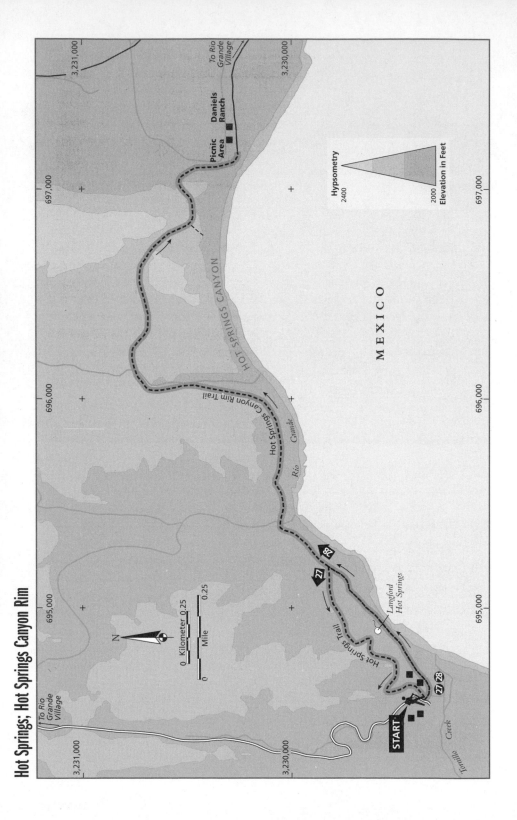

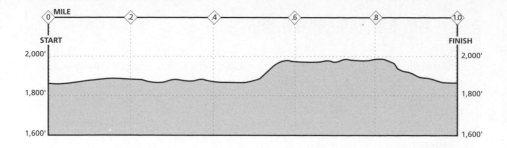

thicket of mesquite, reeds, and other plants before it opens out onto a ledge above the river. The trail follows rock ledges between cliffs above and the river below a short distance to the foundation of the old bathhouse.

The springs still gush out 105-degree water, filling the foundation and creating a popular natural hot tub. The waters still attract bathers many years after Langford first established the resort. On occasion, when the Rio Grande is high, river waters will cover the spring, making bathing impossible. Because of strong currents and hazards made invisible by murky water, the park discourages swimming in the river. In some areas of the West, organisms that live in hot spring water have caused health problems when they enter the body through nasal tissues. To avoid any risk, however slight, avoid getting the water into nasal passages.

Continue the hike by following the trail along the riverbank past the hot spring for about 0.25 mile to a marked junction. Turn left and climb up onto the bluff above the spring. The route contours along the bluff along an old road before dropping back down to the trailhead parking lot from behind the post office. Because of the climb, the return part of the loop is more difficult, but hikers are well rewarded with broad views of the river, mountains, and desert far south in Mexico.

Miles and Directions

- **0.0** Hot Springs parking lot.
- **0.1** Old motel units, pictographs.
- **0.25** Hot spring.
- **0.5** Junction with Hot Springs Canyon Rim Trail. Bear left, up the hill.
- **1.0** End of loop at Hot Springs parking lot.

28 Hot Springs Canyon Rim

General description: A day hike between Langford Hot Springs and Rio Grande Village that overlooks scenic Hot Springs Canyon of the Rio Grande.

Distance: 3 miles one way.

Approximate hiking time: 1.5 hours.

Difficulty: Easy (moderate if done as a round-trip).

Traffic: Heavy to the hot spring, light beyond.

Trail surface: Dirt path.

Topo map: Boquillas.

Finding the trailhead: From park headquarters at Panther Junction, drive a little more than 17 miles along the Rio Grande Village highway to the marked Hot Springs turnoff, on the right. Follow the maintained dirt road 1.7 miles to the parking lot at its end. The last 0.5 mile or so of the road is very narrow and winding and is impassable to RVs, trailers, or very wide vehicles. Drivers of such vehicles will need to park in a parking area on the right side of the road before the narrow, one-way section of road begins. Alternatively, hike the trail in reverse from Daniels Ranch at Rio Grande Village, where any vehicle can park.

The Hike

This trail was improved into an official trail fairly recently, so some maps, including the topographic map, do not show it. The trail starts at the Hot Springs parking lot. Follow the trail down to the river, past the motel and post office built by J. O. Langford in the 1900s as part of his health resort at the springs. After about 0.25 mile, the trail passes the foundations of the bathhouse that he built over the main spring. Except when the river floods it, warm spring water still fills the foundation, creating a tempting hot tub. If this trail is done as a round-trip, a soak in the spring would make a welcome ending to the hike.

About 0.25 mile past the hot spring, the trail forks, with the Hot Springs Trail turning left, up the hill. Stay straight, by the river, on the Hot Springs Canyon Rim Trail. The clearly marked trail crosses a dry drainage and begins to climb up out of the river bottom, but soon drops back down again into a large side canyon. When you reach the bottom of the rocky canyon, look carefully for the trail. It turns right at the bottom, back toward the river; it does not follow the side canyon upstream.

The trail continues along rocky bluffs above the river as Hot Springs Canyon deepens. The route has some ups and downs, but generally climbs steadily higher. With greater height, views open up of the Chisos Mountains, Sierra del Carmen, and Mariscal Mountain. The Rio Grande below becomes an emerald ribbon snaking through endless parched desert. The moisture provided by the river nurtures a lush growth of reeds and grasses on its banks. Wildlife, from deer and white-winged doves to predators such as mountain lions, is drawn by the water, forage, and shelter of the riparian corridor.

Cottonwoods offer welcome shade to hikers at Daniels Ranch, at Rio Grande Village.

About halfway through the hike, the trail turns north, away from the river, to get around a deep side canyon that joins the Rio Grande. Some distance north, the trail is able to cross the side canyon. It climbs back out of the side canyon and begins working its way back to the main river canyon. The trail crosses the high point of the hike and begins its descent back to the river. A short marked overlook side trail offers good views of Hot Springs Canyon. The trail continues to descend for less than 0.5 mile to Rio Grande Village, visible below to the east. The trail ends by the Daniels Ranch, on the west end of the village. The broad, flat river floodplain partly occupied by Rio Grande Village was farmed with cotton and other crops before it became part of the national park in the 1940s.

Today the village has a store, gas station, picnic area, and campground. Tall, shady cottonwoods offer welcome shade after the sunny trail. The hike can easily be done in reverse by starting at Rio Grande Village. With a car shuttle or arranged pick-up, the hike can be done one-way without the need of the return hike. Although the overall elevation gain for this trail is about 360 feet, the actual total amount of climbing is somewhat higher because of the need to cross several side canyons along the way.

Miles and Directions

0.0 Hot Springs parking lot.

0.1 Old motel units, pictographs.

0.25 Hot spring.

0.5 Junction with Hot Springs Canyon Rim Trail.

1.5 Trail leaves river to skirt large side canyon.

2.6 Short side trail to overlook forks to right.

3.0 Rio Grande Village at Daniels Ranch building.

29 Rio Grande Village Nature Trail

General description: A day hike from the Rio Grande Village Campground to the Nature Trail Overlook and back.

Distance: 0.75 mile loop.

Approximate hiking time: 30 minutes.

Difficulty: Easy

Traffic: Heavy.

Trail surface: Boardwalk and dirt path.

Topo map: Boquillas.

Finding the trailhead: The trailhead is located across the road from campsite 18 in the Rio Grande Village Class "A" Campground. Note that parking is limited at the trailhead; park instead near the registration sign for the campground and walk to site 18.

The Hike

The Rio Grande Village Nature Trail is an easy walk that takes the hiker through very diverse ecosystems and shows the different human lifestyles practiced on opposite sides of the Rio Grande. The trail begins with a 150-foot boardwalk that crosses a wetland created by a beaver dam and fed by a warm spring. The abundant spring water allows life for plants and animals not normally associated with desert settings. Willows, reeds, insects, and fish make their home in this special ecosystem. The uncommon habitat is also a haven for many species of birds.

As you climb the hill leaving the spring area, note the dramatic change in the surrounding environment. Not only does the plant life make an abrupt change, turning to desert scrub and cacti, but even the air becomes drier. At the top of the hill, the loop trail forks. Take the trail to the right.

At the next trail junction, only a short distance down the path, you can see the tiny village of Ojo Caliente, Spanish for "hot spring," across the Rio Grande. This village is an *ejido,* a Mexican communal landholding where the agricultural products of the land are owned individually by *ejido* members, although they own the land jointly. As its name implies, a natural hot spring provides water for irrigation at this settlement and makes farming possible. Like the warm spring near the boardwalk, the presence of water at Ojo Caliente creates a moist environment in the desert, allowing the villagers to grow crops sufficient to support themselves and to perhaps trade or sell to nearby settlements.

Take the short spur trail to the right, and walk toward the edge of the Rio Grande. Along the trail, watch for rocks containing the fossils of marine creatures, evidence that this area was once covered by an ancient sea. Farther along, you'll see other signs of past life in the rocks—round, deep mortar holes that were used by prehistoric people to grind seeds, roots, and pods. Just a short distance farther, you'll encounter the Rio Grande, a ribbon of life through the heart of the dry Chihuahuan Desert.

The nature trail offers views of the Rio Grande, the Sierra del Carmen, and the village of Boquillas.

After exploring the riverbank, return to the spur trail junction and continue along the loop to the right. The impressive limestone cliffs rising high above and across the river are part of the mountain range known as the Sierra del Carmen. Located in Mexico, the towering, banded cliffs are visible from many parts of Big Bend National Park.

As you hike up and around the hill, the village of Boquillas del Carmen comes into view. This remote village, near the mouth of Boquillas Canyon, has only a small number of residents. In the early 1900s Boquillas was a booming mining town of about 1,000 people who worked nearby lead, zinc, silver, and fluorite mines. Today, subsistence agriculture supports the residents of Boquillas. Because of border restrictions after the tragedy of September 11, 2001, it is no longer legal to cross over the river to Boquillas.

At the next trail junction, turn left and walk to the top of the hill on another short spur trail. From this high vantage point, enjoy the magnificent panorama spread before you. It includes the Rio Grande, the Chisos Mountains, Rio Grande Village, the Sierra del Carmen, the two Mexican settlements, and vast expanses of Mexico. The difference in lifestyle on opposite sides of the river is evident; the Rio Grande Village Campground with its modern conveniences contrasts with the rural subsistence lifestyle of Ojo Caliente and Boquillas, Mexico. Also evident is the contrast of the lush vegetation of the warm springs and river with the arid Chihuahuan

Desert. The variety of ecosystems and lifestyles along the Rio Grande is what gives the area much of its charm and richness. Now retrace your steps back off the hilltop to the trail junction and turn left. Walk downhill to the next trail junction, the start of the loop, and turn right to return to the campground trailhead.

Miles and Directions

0.0 Trailhead in Rio Grande Village Campground.

0.1 Loop begins at trail junction.

0.2 Spur trail to river goes off to right.

0.4 Spur trail to hilltop goes off to left.

0.65 Loop ends.

0.75 Trailhead in campground.

30 Ore Terminal

General description: A rugged day hike along much of the route of an old ore tramway to its northern terminal.

Distance: 4 miles one way.

Approximate hiking time: 2.5 to 3 hours.

Difficulty: Strenuous.

Traffic: Light to first tramway tower, very light beyond.

Trail surface: Dirt path.

Topo map: Boquillas.

Finding the trailhead: From the junction of the Rio Grande Village road and the Boquillas Canyon road, about 1 mile north of Rio Grande Village, follow the Boquillas Canyon road about 2.8 miles to the marked trailhead on the left side of the road across from a parking area on the right. The trailhead is just past the turnoff for the Boquillas Overlook. Try not to leave valuables in your car; vehicles in this area sometimes suffer break-ins.

The Hike

Between 1909 and 1919, a 6-mile tramway carried ore in ninety ore buckets between the Puerto Rico Mine in the Sierra del Carmen of Mexico and the Texas terminal, the ending point of this hike. When it was operating, the tramway carried 7.5 tons of ore per hour. From the Texas terminal, the silver, lead, and zinc ore was hauled north to the railroad in Marathon. When the mine was abandoned, the tramway was left to rot and rust away. Most of it was built in too rugged a terrain to be economic to salvage. Today the rusting cables snake across the desert along the tramway route. Most of the towers have collapsed, but a number still stand, their decay slowed by the dry climate.

This trail is dry, with very little shade. Late fall to early spring are the best times to do this hike; in summer the hike can be brutal. Carry plenty of water any time

Several old tramway towers still stand along the Ore Terminal Trail.

of year. The trail is lightly used and maintained only irregularly, but is generally not too difficult to follow.

From the parking area, cross the road to the trailhead. The trail heads north up a broad valley into the Dead Horse Mountains. It quickly drops into the dry wash bottom, full of gravel and limestone cobbles. Piles of rocks, or cairns, help mark the route. After about a half mile, the trail climbs up out of the wash on the right side to the first intact wooden tramway tower. The tower is easily visible from the wash on the bench above. The trail follows the rusting cable to other collapsed towers only a short distance away. The trail ahead is easily visible from the towers as it follows the cable up the other side of the canyon wall.

From the towers, take the trail that follows the cable back down into and across the wash to the northwest; do not follow the Strawhouse/Marufo Vega Trail to the right. A sign in the wash also marks the trail split. Begin the steep climb up the Ore Terminal Trail and out of the canyon.

The trail is easy to follow here; rock cairns and the white scratch marks left by mule and horse hooves add further assurance. This section of trail follows the old tram route fairly closely. Collapsed towers, the cable, and ore buckets are obvious

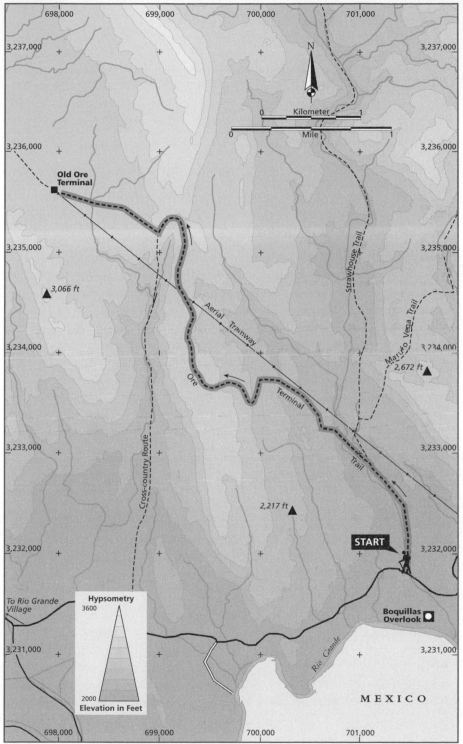

698,000 699,000 700,000 701,000

3,237,000

N

Kilometer
0 1

Mile
0 1

3,236,000

Old Ore Terminal

3,235,000

▲ 3,066 ft

Aerial Tramway

3,234,000

Strawhouse Trail

Maruso Vega Trail

▲ 2,672 ft

Ore

Terminal

Trail

3,233,000

Cross-country Route

▲ 2,217 ft

START

3,232,000

To Rio Grande Village

Hypsometry
3600

Boquillas Overlook □

Rio Grande

3,231,000

2000
Elevation in Feet

MEXICO

698,000 399,000 700,000 701,000

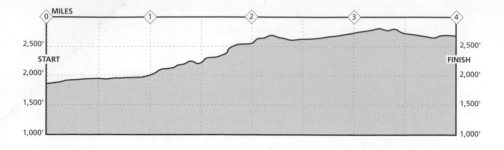

reminders. After climbing over a ridgetop into a small valley, the trail turns west, away from the tram route. Two more standing towers are occasionally visible to the north from the next section of trail.

The trail climbs steeply out of the small valley, up ridges and small canyons until it turns north back toward the tram route. It levels out for 0.5 mile or so as it returns to the tramway route. The trail then follows the tramway a short distance to another standing tower on the brink of a deep canyon that the cable once crossed. Rio Grande Village can be seen far to the south, beyond the mouth of the canyon. A rough trail that descends the far wall of the canyon is visible. This trail is a rugged, unmaintained route to Rio Grande Village that is choked with a lot of brush.

To avoid crossing the deep canyon, the Ore Terminal Trail curves north around its head. After curving around the canyon head, the trail climbs onto a small divide, the highest point of the hike. The wooden remains of the ore terminal itself are visible in the broad valley to the west. The overall route to the terminal is clear, but the trail gets a bit faint in places on this last stretch of trail. The trail descends gradually from the divide to the terminal. Observant hikers may notice the unmarked junction on the left with the route to Rio Grande Village mentioned before, but it is faint. Most hikers will return to the same trailhead; however, it is possible to continue northwest to Old Ore Road.

The massive wooden beams of the ore terminal still remain solid, although the entire structure leans. Pieces of ore lie on the ground, along with rusting cans, bolts, and other debris. Please do not take any artifacts or rocks.

A heavy sense of isolation hangs over the terminal ruins; no other sign of man can be seen in the broad sweep of desert and mountains. The miners are long gone; only the wind whistling around the wooden beams provides company.

Miles and Directions

0.0 Ore Terminal trailhead.

0.5 First standing tramway tower.

0.8 Trail begins climb out of canyon and splits from Strawhouse/Marufo Vega Trail.

3.4 Highest point of trail.

3.5 Junction with little-used Rio Grande Village Trail.

4.0 Old ore terminal.

31 Boquillas Canyon

General description: A day hike into the entrance of Boquillas Canyon, one of three major canyons in Big Bend National Park carved by the Rio Grande.

Distance: 0.7 mile one way.

Approximate hiking time: 30 minutes.

Difficulty: Easy.

Traffic: Heavy.

Trail surface: Dirt path.

Topo map: Boquillas.

Finding the trailhead: From park headquarters at Panther Junction, drive about 20 miles southeast toward Rio Grande Village. Turn left onto the Boquillas Canyon road just before entering Rio Grande Village and drive 4 miles to the parking lot at the end of the road, where the trail begins. Vehicle break-ins are occasionally a problem here, so do not leave any valuables in your car.

The Hike

The word Boquillas means "little mouths" in Spanish. Although no one is sure where the name for the canyon originated, some believe it was named either for the canyon's narrow entrance or for the numerous small openings, or solution holes, in its limestone walls. The Boquillas Canyon Trail is a popular short trail, appropriate for adults and children. Be aware, however, that during late spring, summer, and early fall midday temperatures frequently rise above 100 degrees Fahrenheit. During the hot time of year, walks along this trail are best taken in the early morning hours.

From the parking area, the trail immediately climbs about 50 feet onto a low ridge then levels off as the Rio Grande comes into view. The route is lined with typical Chihuahuan Desert vegetation such as creosote bush, lechuguilla, leatherstem,

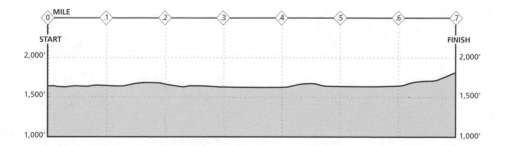

ocotillo, and several varieties of prickly pear cactus. A few yards further on, the trail splits. If you go to the right, you will skirt a small hill and descend toward the river. Choose the left-hand path to climb up a slight rise and discover an excellent view of the Rio Grande and the entrance to Boquillas Canyon. Looking west from here, you can see the village of Boquillas, Mexico, across the river. About 175 people inhabit the former mining town.

The short left-hand trail rejoins the main trail a bit down the hill via a series of steep log steps. The trail takes you down about 90 feet to the banks of the Rio Grande. Upon reaching the river level, the main trail turns to the left, or east. Walk right, or west, for about 50 feet, however, and you find yourself on a rock ledge in which there are several mortar holes made by prehistoric people who once lived in this area. Mortar holes like these, used for grinding seeds, roots, and pods, can be found throughout Big Bend. Although the exact age of the mortar holes is unknown, their presence near desert springs and the river underscores the importance of reliable water sources to former inhabitants.

Returning to the main trail, you parallel the river and wind through tunnels of river cane, primarily non-native giant reed. Some of the smaller, native common reed is mixed in; distinguish the two by looking for the erect seedheads of the non-native and the drooping seedheads of the native cane. This section of the trail can be washed out or impassable at times due to river flooding, especially in late summer and early fall. Here and everywhere along the river, be careful if you walk along the banks. The river's surface hides deep holes and strong undercurrents.

The trail opens up to a large rocky beach at the edge of the Rio Grande in the entrance to this magnificent limestone canyon. Directly ahead, notice the fault line in the limestone cliff on the Mexican side of the river; it is obvious where the left-hand side of the fault dropped in relation to the right side.

Note the huge sand slide heaped up against the canyon wall on the American side. Down-canyon winds created it by piling loose sand against the rocks. The slide is fun to climb, but quite strenuous. A shallow cave in the canyon wall tops the slide. Downstream of the rocky beach, further travel stops where the river cuts off the beach and flows against the canyon wall. To return to the parking lot, retrace your steps.

Miles and Directions

0.0 Boquillas Canyon trailhead.
0.7 End of trail where Rio Grande cuts off riverbank.

◀ *A hiker stands by the river in the mouth of Boquillas Canyon.*

Boquillas Canyon

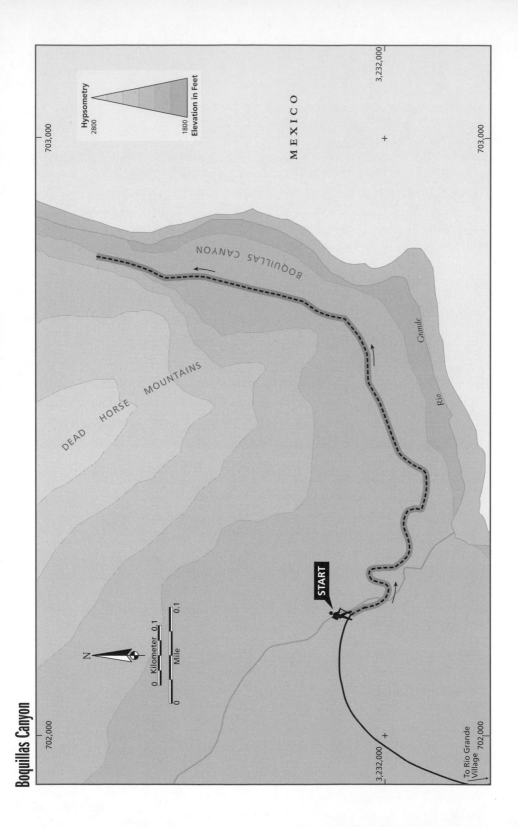

MEXICO

3,232,000

703,000

703,000

Hypsometry
2800

Elevation in Feet
1800

BOQUILLAS CANYON

DEAD HORSE MOUNTAINS

Rio Grande

N

0   Kilometer   0.1

0   Mile   0.1

START

To Rio Grande
Village

702,000

702,000

3,232,000

32 Marufo Vega

General description: A backpack or strenuous day hike through the Dead Horse Mountains to the rim of Boquillas Canyon or the Rio Grande.
Distance: Up to 14 miles out and back.
Approximate hiking time: Up to 8 hours out and back.
Difficulty: Strenuous.
Traffic: Light to moderate.
Trail surface: Dirt path.
Topo maps: Boquillas, Ernst Valley.

Finding the trailhead: From the junction of the Rio Grande Village road and the Boquillas Canyon road, about 1 mile north of Rio Grande Village, follow the Boquillas Canyon road about 2.8 miles to the marked trailhead on the left side of the road across from a parking area on the right. The trailhead is just past the turnoff for the Boquillas Overlook. The Marufo Vega trailhead is the same as the Strawhouse and Ore Terminal trailheads. Try not to leave valuables in your car; this area sometimes suffers break-ins.

The Hike

The Marufo Vega Trail offers a strenuous but spectacular trip with a variety of hiking options in the Dead Horse Mountains, including the rim of Boquillas Canyon and the Rio Grande. About 3.5 miles into this rugged hike, the trail splits into south and north forks. The north fork descends a steep canyon drainage and reaches the river in about 2.5 more miles. From the junction the south fork leads to the Rio Grande in a little more than 3 miles, plus provides excellent views from the heights of the canyon rim. The last mile of the south fork drops very abruptly to the river. A 1.5-mile connecting trail joins the ends of each Marufo Vega fork by traveling parallel to and above the river.

The total round-trip distance from the trailhead to the river by way of the south fork, then down the river via the connecting trail to the north fork, and then returning to the trailhead via the north fork is roughly 14 miles. For a long day hike to the river, consider a round-trip trek on the north fork; for a long day hike to the canyon rim, consider hiking the south fork about 5 miles to the rim. To do any part of this trail requires good experience and fitness, and only the most fit and experienced should try to do the entire loop in one day. For an overnight trip to the river, consider hiking down the south fork and up the north fork, the route described here. Another option would be to set up a base camp along the first stretch of the Marufo Vega Trail, thus making for a shorter and less strenuous hike to the river the following day.

Avoid the Marufo Vega Trail from April through September. There is no water and limited shade until you reach the river. Afternoon temperatures commonly exceed 100 degrees Fahrenheit. Although there is water in the Rio Grande, it is of dubious quality even if purified. Topographic maps are essential. The Big Bend Trails Illustrated map does not show the trail correctly and is not adequate for the hike. The park also has a helpful free hand-out map of the trail.

The Marufo Vega Trail offers seldom seen views of the Sierra del Carmen.

In March or early April, pack a wildflower field guide with you to identify the many blooms dotting the route. The delicate and colorful flowers contrast sharply with the rugged landscape. Late September and October are also ideal times to hike this area as vegetation comes to life after the summer thunderstorms. Grasses and shrubs turn green and autumn wildflowers make their appearance.

From the trailhead, look northward toward the cliffs of the Dead Horse Mountains. In the distance, a gap cutting through the cliffs marks the direction in which you will be heading. Initially, the Marufo Vega/Strawhouse/Ore Terminal Trail follows a large dry wash north for almost a mile, where you encounter the ruins of the old ore tramway. While still in the drainage bottom, the route splits just as it crosses the tramway route, marked by a rusty fallen steel cable and collapsing wooden towers. The Ore Terminal Trail forks left and ascends the hills on the western side of the valley. The marked Marufo Vega/Strawhouse Trail goes right and climbs out of the drainage bottom toward a gap cut by the drainage into the cliffs of the Dead Horse Mountains.

As the trail creeps upward and into the gap, it follows a geologic formation of sparkling crystals. The opaque, brownish white calcite crystals almost pave the route;

they glitter brightly in sharp contrast to the surrounding monotonous limestone layers. Once inside the gap, watch for the sign that marks the junction where the Marufo Vega Trail leaves the Strawhouse Trail.

While the Strawhouse Trail continues north through the pass, the Marufo Vega Trail turns right and switchbacks up the steep slope forming the east side of the gap. The trail steepens considerably and gains several hundred feet in a very short distance. The great views from the top of this climb provide some consolation for the effort. The ore tramway valley extends to the northwest; Ernst Valley to the north. To the south, Mexico lies beyond the meandering Rio Grande valley with the village of Boquillas hugging the water's edge. The first view of El Pico, the prominent high peak of the Sierra del Carmen in Mexico, appears from just down the trail from the top of the climb.

The trail turns north as it gently descends through typical Chihuahuan Desert habitat and the consistently tilted geology of the Dead Horse Mountains. This area provides some relatively level terraces for setting up a camp if desired. In about 0.5 mile from the top of the climb, a metal sign marks a trail leading off to the left. This northwest-heading spur leads back down into Ernst Valley and connects with the Strawhouse Trail. Remember this junction so that you will not be confused on your return trip.

Within less than 0.5 mile, the Marufo Vega Trail drops into an arroyo and then follows the rocky drainage upstream. The trail drops into, through, and out of the drainage many times. Use the map and watch carefully to stay on the proper route. The walls of this small canyon drainage not only provide scattered shade, they also afford a close-up look at the massive limestone Del Carmen Formation. These geologic layers, forming the bulk of Boquillas Canyon, consist solely of limestone rock created eons ago by microscopic organisms in ancient seas.

After climbing slowly through the winding drainage for about a mile, the trail splits. Follow your map closely as the north fork continues north, out of the main arroyo, while the south fork stays in the drainage and turns east. In less than 0.5 mile, the south fork also leads out of the drainage. However, before you follow the trail out of the drainage, walk another 100 feet up the drainage to an unexpected sight. Long ago, someone built a dam in this unnamed arroyo lying within the heart of the Dead Horse Mountains. Small in size and completely silted in, the structure marks a futile attempt to tame this rugged land.

From the arroyo, the route easily traverses a small basin rimmed by cliffs several hundred feet high. Gradually, the trail climbs into a small pass lying at 2,800 feet, and soon after a view opens up of Boquillas Canyon. Because Boquillas is more heavily eroded than the park's other canyons, it lacks the sheer-walled, narrow-canyon character of the others. Instead, this area resembles a small-scale Grand Canyon with alternating cliffs and plateaus stepping down from the rim to the river floodplain. Deep side canyons dissect Boquillas Canyon's limestone walls, while pinnacles jut upward from its rugged contours. The south fork remains at roughly

Marufo Vega

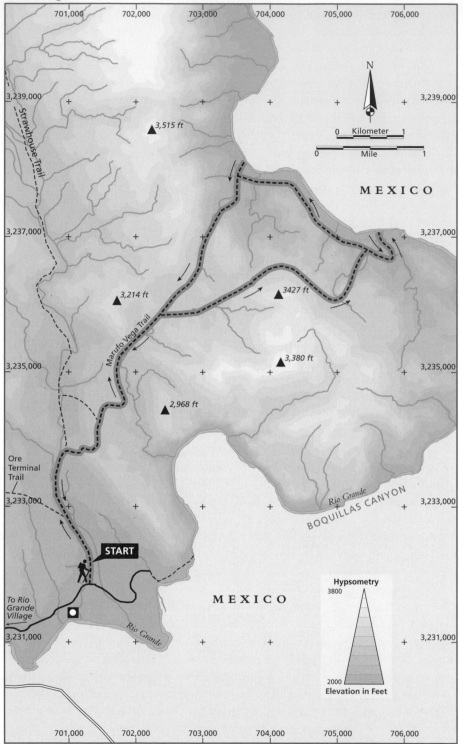

the same elevation for about another mile, offering some spectacular views, particularly at sunrise and sunset.

The trail begins its descent to the Rio Grande at a total distance of about 5 miles from the trailhead. The next mile is steep, with unsure footing on a loose rocky surface. Use caution as you descend, especially if you are carrying a heavy backpack. This section of the Marufo Vega Trail was constructed long ago without much regard for angle of descent or switchbacks. For the most part, the trail simply follows the steep grade straight downhill.

As you approach the Rio Grande, the trail splits. The right fork continues down to the river, reaching it in about 0.5 mile. There are some good campsites along the floodplain at the end of the trail. The left fork parallels the Rio Grande and follows it downstream for a little more than a mile. It connects with the north fork of the Marufo Vega Trail, which also leads down to the river and to some nice campsites. If you intend to camp along the river, plan to do so where either the north or south forks of the trail lead down to the Rio Grande; the connecting trail lies high above the river and provides no easy access to it.

To return, either retrace your route back along the south fork of the trail or take the connecting trail to the north fork. From the junction of the north fork and the connecting trail near the river, the north fork ascends to the southwest through a narrow-walled side canyon. Although the route is steep, the trail is easier than the south fork. The canyon cliffs generate refreshing shade, and breezes through the passage are common. Midway along the route, Texas persimmon, sumac, and other large shrubs combine with rock walls and small pour-offs to create a grotto-like scene.

Once you reach the top of the canyon, the north fork continues for about 0.5 mile to the junction with the south fork encountered earlier in the hike. From this point, the trailhead is still about 3.5 miles distant—but most of the return is either downhill or level.

Miles and Directions

0.0 Combined Marufo Vega/Strawhouse/Ore Terminal trailhead.

0.5 First standing tramway tower.

0.8 Strawhouse/Marufo Vega Trail splits to the right from Ore Terminal Trail and begins climb out of canyon bottom.

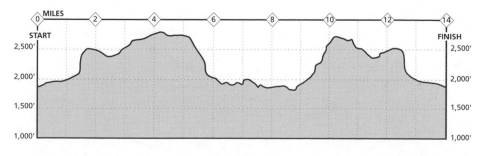

1.4 Marufo Vega Trail forks right from Strawhouse Trail in gap.

1.8 Top of main climb.

2.2 Junction with unnamed trail that connects with Strawhouse Trail. Stay right.

3.5 Trail junction. To make the complete loop, turn right onto the south fork.

5.0 South fork begins steep descent into canyon.

6.0 Connecting trail splits off to left to meet with north fork.

6.5 Rio Grande at end of south fork.

7.0 Junction of south fork and connecting trail.

8.5 Junction of connection trail and north fork.

8.75 Rio Grande at end of north fork.

9.0 Junction of connecting trail and north fork.

10.5 Junction of north and south forks.

14.0 Arrive back at the trailhead.

33 Telephone Canyon

General description: A primitive backpack from Old Ore Road over the high ridges of the Dead Horse Mountains to the eastern park boundary with the Adams Ranch.
Distance: 16.7 miles one way.
Approximate hiking time: 8.5 to 9 hours.

Difficulty: Strenuous and difficult to follow.
Traffic: Very light.
Trail surface: Dirt path and sand, gravel, and cobbles of dry desert wash.
Topo maps: Roys Peak, Ernst Valley, Sue Peaks, McKinney Springs, Stillwell Crossing.

Finding the trailhead: The Telephone Canyon trailhead lies at the end of a 0.25-mile spur road about 14 miles from the south end of Old Ore Road. Because reaching the east trailhead at the Adams Ranch requires crossing private land, ask a ranger for information before using the eastern trailhead. High-clearance, four-wheel-drive vehicles are often necessary to reach either trailhead.

The Strawhouse Trail begins on the Boquillas Canyon road and joins the Telephone Canyon Trail about 10 miles from Old Ore Road.

The Hike

This description assumes the hiker is traveling west to east from Old Ore Road to the Adams Ranch. There is no water along this trail; carry plenty. Because summer temperatures often exceed 100 degrees Fahrenheit, this is not a hike for the hot months of the year.

This is a long, strenuous hike on a little-used trail that is often difficult to follow. Only strong, knowledgeable hikers should attempt it. Gain experience on other eas–

Telephone Canyon

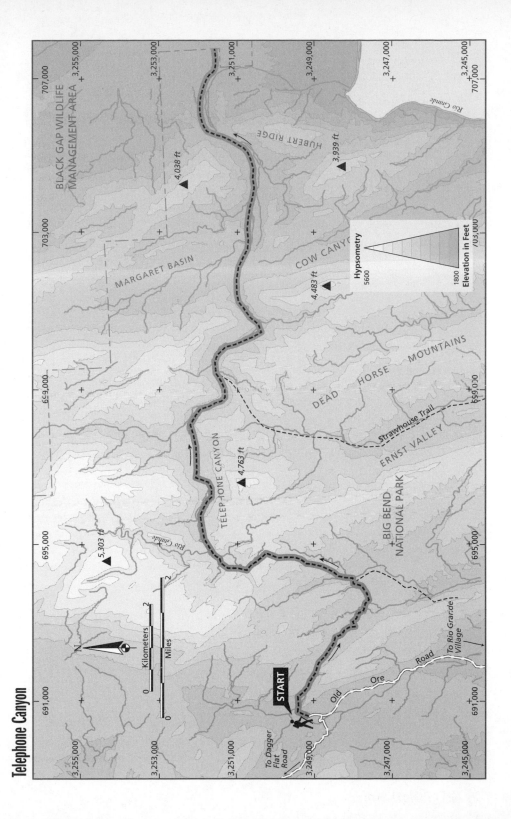

ier desert trails in the park before trying this one. Good map-reading and route-finding skills are needed. In this area, every hill and side canyon can look alike.

Permission must be obtained from the Adams Ranch in order to use the eastern trailhead as a starting point or for a car shuttle. Talk to park rangers for information about using the eastern trailhead. Please respect private property.

The first section of trail by Old Ore Road briefly enters an arroyo near the north end of Alto Relex, then climbs left up a limestone slope studded with cacti and thorny brush. The trail is marked with rock cairns and is fairly easy to follow toward the top of the pass. The rock dam near the top is a good destination for a short day hike. The small dam is similar to many scattered throughout the park, reminders of early settlers' struggle to capture enough water to survive. How long until the next rain fills the catch basin?

For the next few miles, you may need to use topo maps to locate landmarks. The route leads southeast into a secluded valley, winds down an eroded slope, then turns northeast to cross low hills. The junction on the right with a trail from Ernst Basin is marked with a large cairn in the drainage east of the hills. The Telephone Canyon Trail goes upstream and soon climbs out of the arroyo on the east, or right side. The trail climbs to the top of the next ridge, about 1.5 miles away and 1,200 feet higher. Small cairns and scratches on the rocks left by livestock help mark the way.

As you climb, watch for subtle changes in vegetation. Gregg's ash, palo prieto, and leadtree appear. Sotols and giant yuccas, or daggers, are numerous farther up, and dwarf oaks are found on the highest ridges. The view from the top reveals a vast desert wilderness below and on all sides, with distant blue mountains, including the Chisos, forming the horizon. Sue Peaks, the highest points in the Dead Horse Range, are to the north.

The trail turns northwest and descends along the left side of a drainage, finally curving east and dropping steeply into Telephone Canyon. From this point, the trail is unmarked. However, it follows the bottom of the canyon all the way to Hubert Ridge, about 9 miles away. Pick the best path through the clumps of walnut trees and brush and continue downstream. In some places, the canyon walls rise over 800 feet.

After a few canyon turns, Heath Creek enters from the north. Like Margaret

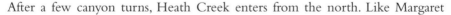

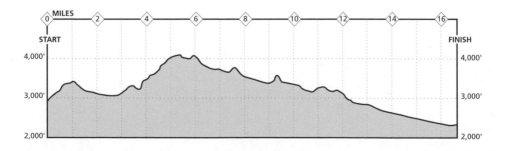

Basin, North Telephone Canyon, and other valleys the trail passes, the Heath Creek area is almost never visited by hikers.

The junction with the Strawhouse Trail is marked with several large rock cairns along the right, or south, side of the drainage. The Strawhouse Trail climbs up and into a small canyon toward the Boquillas Canyon road, about 14 miles away.

Telephone Canyon gradually becomes more open and increasingly the vegetation becomes more desert-like. Finally, after a sharp turn around Hubert Ridge, the trail climbs out of the drainage onto the left, or north side, where it meets an old ranch road. Follow the road downhill to a fenced gate at the eastern trailhead. The gate marks the Adams Ranch boundary, and the limit of vehicle access.

Miles and Directions

0.0 Trailhead at Old Ore Road. Trail climbs east.

0.9 Rock dam.

1.1 Top of pass.

2.8 Trail turns northeast, crosses low hill.

3.4 Meets trail to Ernst Basin in arroyo bottom.

4.8 Crosses top of ridge. Highest elevation of trail.

6.4 Reaches bottom of Telephone Canyon.

9.1 Heath Creek drainage enters from north.

10.3 Rock cairn marks junction with Strawhouse Trail.

13.2 Margaret Basin drainage enters from north.

13.9 North Telephone Canyon enters from north.

14.6 Unnamed canyon enters from south.

15.2 Hubert Ridge. Trail leaves bottom of drainage, climbs north (left when facing downstream) bank.

15.5 Meets old ranch road near water tank (dry).

16.7 Private property begins, limit of vehicle access via the Adams Ranch. Be sure to close the gate.

34 Strawhouse

General description: A primitive route through the rugged Dead Horse Mountains between the Boquillas Canyon road and the Telephone Canyon Trail.

Distance: 14 miles one way.

Approximate hiking time: 7 to 8 hours.

Difficulty: Strenuous, with some difficulty in route-finding.

Traffic: Very light except for first mile at southern end.

Trail surface: Dirt path and sand, gravel, and cobbles of dry desert wash.

Topo maps: Sue Peaks, Ernst Valley, Boquillas.

Finding the trailhead: To start at the north trailhead, follow the Telephone Canyon Trail (the Telephone Canyon trailhead lies at the end of a 0.25-mile spur road about 13 miles from the south end of Old Ore Road) for about 10 miles from its western trailhead to the junction with the Strawhouse Trail. You will need the Sue Peaks topographic map to find the junction. To start this hike from the south, take the Boquillas Canyon road for 2.8 miles from its start at the north edge of Rio Grande Village to the trailhead just past the turnoff for the Boquillas Overlook. Park in the pullout on the right; the marked trail starts right across the road. This is the trailhead for the Ore Terminal Trail and the Marufo Vega Trail as well as the Strawhouse Trail. This area sometimes suffers break-ins; be sure to leave no valuables in your car.

The Hike

The Strawhouse Trail, named for a house made of river cane and candelilla stems that once stood at the river near the southern end of the trail, is one of Big Bend's most remote routes. This 14-mile primitive use trail (really more a route than a developed trail) runs from its junction with the Telephone Canyon Trail to the Boquillas Canyon road. The route follows a broad north-south drainage. Hiking consists largely of rocky or sandy wash walking with the exception of the northernmost 1.25 miles, which require careful route-finding through dense vegetation. The 7.5-minute USGS topographic maps listed above are important tools, very necessary for this hike. There is no water to be found along this route; all water must be carried with you. Because this hike is usually very hot from mid–April to mid–October, it is best done during the cooler months of the year.

This trail description follows the trail from north to south. As you turn south onto the Strawhouse Trail from its junction with the Telephone Canyon Trail, you enter a narrow drainage choked with vegetation. For the first 1.25 miles, you will be climbing uphill to a small pass. This section of the route is very difficult; although you are following the drainage, you cannot walk in the wash because of dense vegetation. You will be better off if you walk above the drainage on the west side, but even there you will be forced to walk through lechuguilla, sotol, and catclaw acacia. Long pants are a must, and long sleeves are helpful. Don't despair; although this section can take about 1.5 hours to negotiate, it is relatively short and travel gets much

The canyon followed by the Strawhouse Trail narrows near the Marufo Vega Trail junctions.

easier once you complete it. Toward the end of this section, you may find traces of an old, faint trail on the west side of the drainage, which makes the going easier.

Once over the small pass, the vegetation thins. You will be able to walk easily on either side of the drainage until it clears out enough for you to walk in the wash itself. The wash at this upper end is rocky and still quite narrow; as you head south it widens into the Ernst Valley and becomes sandy, giving your calf muscles a good workout.

About 2.25 miles down the trail you will see signs of a fire that began on April 21, 1989, and burned 1,268 acres of sotol, yucca, brush, and grass. Lightning set the fire; it burned for four days before it went out on its own. Signs of the fire can be seen for approximately 1.5 miles in the form of charred vegetation on the east side of the trail.

As you walk through the broad valley, you will see caves in the limestone walls above you that, in some cases, were inhabited by prehistoric people in earlier days. Lack of water must have made this a difficult place to live. Possibly early inhabitants used this area only during the wet season. Remember, no collecting of any kind is

Strawhouse

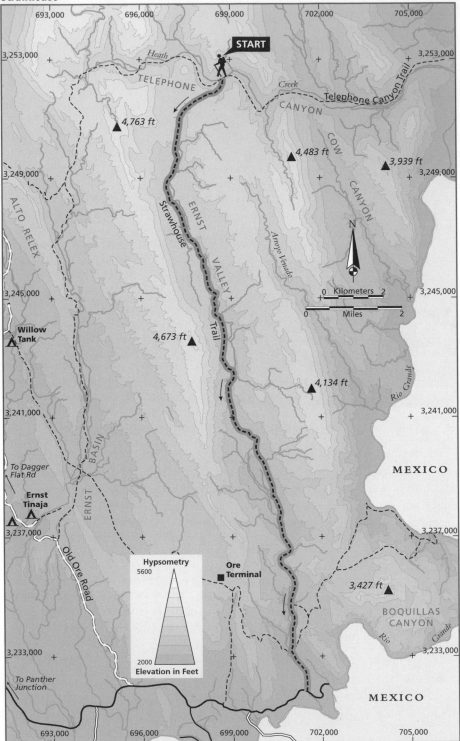

allowed in the park; all objects must be left where found and archaeological sites left undisturbed.

About 6.5 miles down the route you will come to a section of wash about 1.5 miles in length where you will have to climb down and around large boulders. Although the Ernst Valley topographic map shows the trail temporarily leaving the wash in this area and in another spot farther south, the turnoffs are difficult to find. You will probably be better off simply staying in the wash and negotiating through the boulders. This is not too difficult if you are heading north to south because you are following a slight downhill grade.

After you are through the boulder section, the wash returns to its sandy condition and is easy to follow. In about 2 miles you come to a winding canyon; about 2 miles beyond it, you walk through another short canyon with very narrow walls. This is only about 1.5 miles from the end of the trail. In this area, you will pass two turnoffs of the Marufo Vega Trail on the east side of the Strawhouse Trail; the northern junction is north of the narrow canyon, the southern turnoff is south of the canyon. In another 0.25 mile, you will see where the Ore Terminal Trail forks off to the right (west). An old tramway tower can be seen on the bench above the wash to the east from this point. From here it is a little more than 0.5 mile to where the trail leaves the wash on the right, or west side. Exit the wash here and follow the short connecting trail to the Boquillas Canyon road and the parking area.

Miles and Directions

0.0 North trailhead at junction with Telephone Canyon Trail.

1.25 Small pass between Telephone Canyon and Ernst Valley.

2.25 Begin passing site of 1989 fire.

6.5 Boulders in wash create obstacles for about next 1.5 miles.

10.7 Valley narrows to winding canyon.

12.0 A fork of the Marufo Vega Trail climbs out of the canyon to the east.

12.5 Canyon followed by trail becomes very narrow.

13.0 Second Marufo Vega Trail fork climbs out of canyon to the east.

13.2 Ore Terminal Trail climbs out of valley to the west.

14.0 Trailhead at Boquillas Canyon road.

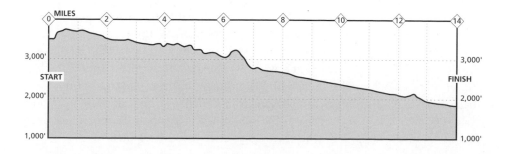

35 Ernst Basin Complex Overview

The desert valley known as Ernst Basin is hidden between rugged limestone ridges of the Dead Horse Mountains. These seldom-used routes through the basin offer a chance to experience the silent beauty of a true desert wilderness and view the highly adapted varieties of plants and animals that live within it.

There is no water in Ernst Basin and very little shade. The area is very hot during summer months, making late fall through early spring the best times to hike here. High-clearance or four-wheel-drive vehicles may be needed to reach the trailheads. Be sure to check with a ranger about road conditions before beginning your trip.

35a Ernst Basin—Willow Tank

General description: A day hike or backpack from Old Ore Road near Ernst Tinaja through Ernst Basin to Willow Tank.
Distance: 5.5 miles one way.
Approximate hiking time: 2.5 to 3 hours.
Difficulty: Moderate to strenuous, with some route-finding required.
Traffic: Very light.
Trail surface: Dirt path, partly sand, gravel, and cobbles of dry desert wash, partly old abandoned dirt road, and partly cross-country.
Topo maps: San Vicente, Roys Peak.

Finding the trailhead: Follow Old Ore Road about 3.5 miles from its south end to a closed spur road that forks right, east, from Old Ore Road. This closed road is the trail. Be sure not to block the Ernst Tinaja 2 campsite when you park. Willow Tank, the north trailhead, is about 10 miles from the south end of Old Ore Road. Old Ore Road turns north off the road to Rio Grande Village about 18 miles from Panther Junction.

The Hike

Begin hiking by following the ruts of a closed road to the top of Cuesta Carlota, near Ernst Tinaja. As you walk, imagine a team of mules struggling to pull a wagon up the slope or picture yourself driving up it in a Model T. The highest point of the cuesta, or ridge, is a great destination for a picnic. The views are worth the short climb even if you do not continue hiking into Ernst Basin.

While enjoying the view from the high point, use your topographic maps to plan the route ahead. Note the location of the junction of the three Ernst Basin trails within the dry arroyos to the northeast. From the top of the ridge, the trail angles down to the left. At the bottom, it stays along the base of the ridge until it reaches the gravel arroyo near the mouth of Ernst Tinaja Canyon. The trail is not well marked beyond this point. Go upstream in the drainage, consult your map, and watch for the rock cairn that marks the trail junction. At the junction, the correct trail turns northwest, or left, when facing upstream, and leaves the arroyo.

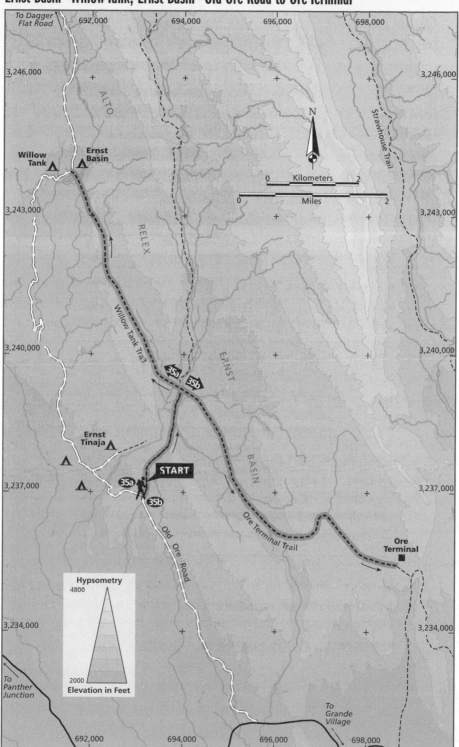

The trail soon enters another drainage to follow the traces of the original Ore Road. Used first as a ranch road to a nearby stock tank, it was improved and extended to the Ore Terminal around 1914. The scant rainfall collects along the tracks of the road, enabling very dense tangles of thorny brush to grow. Where the brush is too thick to penetrate, work your way around the tangles, and pick up the trail again on the other side.

The valley narrows near its upper end, and the trail leaves the drainage toward the northwest, or left when facing upstream, to cross a low divide. It soon takes a turn to the west and arrives at the Willow Tank and Ernst Basin campsites on the Old Ore Road. This hike may be done as a loop by hiking back to the start along the Old Ore Road. A car shuttle greatly shortens the hike.

Miles and Directions

0.0 Trailhead on Old Ore Road. Trail climbs northeast on closed road.

1.2 Side trail to rim of Ernst Tinaja Canyon.

1.4 Top of Cuesta Carlota; trail descends into Ernst Basin.

1.8 Trail enters drainage upstream of Ernst Tinaja Canyon.

2.3 Trail junction. Turn left and follow old road northwest.

2.7 Trail enters smaller, brush-filled drainage.

5.1 Trail leaves the drainage and crosses a low pass on old road.

5.3 Gate marks limit of vehicle access.

5.5 North trailhead at Ernst Basin and Willow Tank campsites on Old Ore Road.

35b Ernst Basin—Old Ore Road to Ore Terminal

General description: A day hike or backpack from Old Ore Road near Ernst Tinaja through Ernst Basin to the Ore Terminal.
Distance: 6.1 miles one way.
Approximate hiking time: 3 hours.
Difficulty: Moderate to strenuous.

Traffic: Very light.
Trail surface: Dirt path, partly sand, gravel, and cobbles of dry desert wash, partly old abandoned dirt road, and partly cross-country.
Topo maps: Boquillas, Ernst Valley, San Vicente, Roys Peak.

Finding the trailhead: Follow Old Ore Road about 3.5 miles from its south end to a closed spur road that forks right, east, from Old Ore Road. This closed road is the trail. The Willow Tank, Ore Terminal, and Telephone Canyon hikes share the same trailhead and first 2.3 miles of trail.

The Hike

Begin hiking by following the ruts of a closed road to the top of Cuesta Carlota, near East Tinaja. From the high point of Cuesta Carlota, note the location of the trail junction inside Ernst Basin. Then look for an old road leading southeast from the junction. This road is the trail to the Ore Terminal.

A short distance after leaving the junction at mile 2.3, the route turns eastward around the end of a ridge, then again turns southeast, and winds through low hills before entering another valley. Beyond this point the trail is almost flat. It is easier to follow than other basin routes and is also delightfully free of the thorny growth found in other parts of the basin.

The incredible jumble of timbers and enormous metal gears that once was the three-story Ore Terminal are at the south end of the valley at the end of the old road. From 1909 to 1919, a 6-mile tramway carried 7.5 tons of silver, lead, and zinc ore per hour from a Mexican mine to this terminal. In today's deep silence, it is hard to imagine a time when the terminal was loud with the sounds of machinery and busy human activity. Consider the difficulties of life for man and beast who lived and worked in such a remote, hot, and dry spot.

The high, scenic ridges above the trail, the absence of artificial lights within view, and the serenity of empty desert make this an enjoyable destination for overnight trips. Rather than returning to the Old Ore Road trailhead, this hike may be extended to the Boquillas Canyon road via the Ore Terminal Trail. To do such a combination, some sort of shuttle will need to be arranged ahead of time.

Miles and Directions

0.0 Trailhead on Old Ore Road. Trail climbs northeast on old closed road.
1.2 Side trail to rim of Ernst Tinaja Canyon.
1.4 Top of Cuesta Carlota; trail descends into Ernst Basin.
1.8 Trail enters drainage upstream of Ernst Tinaja Canyon.
2.3 Trail junction. Turn right and follow an old road southeast.
3.1 Trail turns eastward and passes the end of a ridge.
3.6 Trail turns southeast and enters different valley.
6.1 The ore terminal.

35c Ernst Basin—Telephone Canyon

General description: A cross-country backpack from Old Ore Road near Ernst Tinaja to the western Telephone Canyon trailhead.
Distance: 10.9 or 12.8 miles one way.
Approximate hiking time: 5.5 to 7 hours.
Difficulty: Strenuous, with some difficulty in route-finding.
Trail surface: Dirt path, partly sand, gravel and cobbles of dry desert wash, partly old abandoned dirt road, and partly cross-country.
Topo maps: San Vicente, Roys Peak, Ernst Valley.

Finding the trailhead: Follow Old Ore Road about 3.5 miles from its south end to a closed spur road that forks right, east, from Old Ore Road. This closed road is the trail. The Willow Tank Ore Terminal, and Telephone Canyon hikes share the same trailhead and first 2.3 miles of trail. The northern trailhead, the Telephone Canyon trailhead, is about fourteen miles from the south end of Old Ore Road.

The Hike

Although this trail is shown on topographic maps, it is no more than a route through a remote area. No marked trail exists between Ernst Basin and the Telephone Canyon Trail. The most direct route described in the mileage log and the description below is not marked on maps. The unmarked route is about 2 miles shorter.

Begin hiking by following the ruts of a closed road to the top of Cuesta Carlota, near East Tinaja. From the high point of Cuesta Carlota, hikers should note the location of the trail junction in the basin and identify Alto Relex Mountain to the north.

Beyond the junction at mile 2.3, continue hiking up the arroyo to the southern tip of Alto Relex. The walls of the arroyo rise to form a delightfully shaded canyon at the southeast end of Alto Relex Mountain.

After passing through the canyon, the drainage continues its slow climb within the hidden folds of the Dead Horse Range. The grass- and lechuguilla-covered slopes bake in the sun. No trace of man is visible; months may pass before the next hiker walks by.

The direct route to the Old Ore Road stays in the drainage near the base of Alto Relex, eventually meeting the Telephone Canyon Trail in a pass near the north end of the mountain. Study your topographic maps closely if you choose to hike the longer route. After leaving the canyon, several drainages enter from the east, and there are no markers to indicate which one the route follows. A wrong choice could lead into a maze of box canyons, so if in doubt, take the shorter route.

A few large piles of rocks stacked in an arroyo bottom mark where the longer route joins the Telephone Canyon Trail. Turn left when facing upstream and climb the Telephone Canyon Trail out of the arroyo. The trail is indistinct across the top of some low hills, but watch for small cairns marking the way. Once you reach an arroyo at the bottom of a hill, turn right toward the pass on the north end of Alto Relex. Although the trail winds through thick brush in the arroyo, it is marked with cairns.

The top of the pass is a great place to drop your pack for a break, and look back into the area you've just come through. How much time will pass before the next hiker comes along? How long since the last rain made the valley green?

The remaining mile of trail to Old Ore Road is all downhill and marked with cairns. With a car shuttle, this hike can be done as a long, strenuous day hike. Otherwise, it is best done as a backpack.

Miles and Directions

0.0 Trailhead on Old Ore Road. Trail climbs northeast on old closed road.

1.2 Side trail to rim of Ernst Tinaja Canyon.

1.4 Top of Cuesta Carlota; trail descends into Ernst Basin.

1.8 Trail enters drainage upstream of Ernst Tinaja Canyon.

Ernst Basin–Telephone Canyon

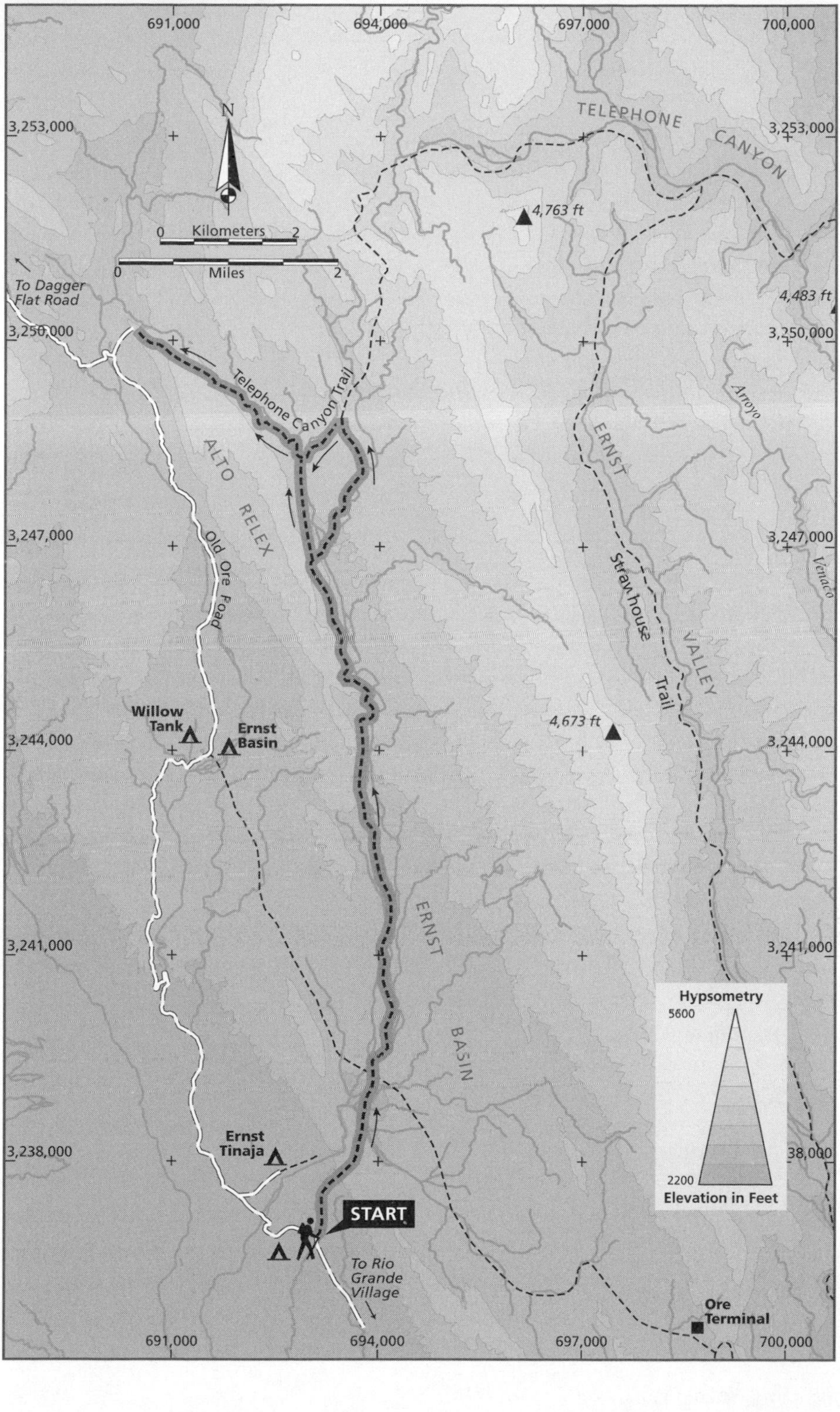
691,000
694,000
697,000
700,000
3,253,000
3,250,000
3,247,000
3,244,000
3,241,000
3,238,000
N
0 Kilometers 2
0 Miles 2
To Dagger Flat Road
TELEPHONE CANYON
4,763 ft
4,483 ft
Telephone Canyon Trail
ALTO RELEX
Old Ore Road
ERNST
Strawhouse Trail
VALLEY
Arroyo
Venado
Willow Tank
Ernst Basin
4,673 ft
ERNST BASIN
Ernst Tinaja
START
To Rio Grande Village
Hypsometry
5600
2200
Elevation in Feet
Ore Terminal

2.3 Trail junction. This trail stays in the drainage; do not turn right or left.

4.8 Trail enters a canyon near south end of Alto Relex.

6.6 Canyon ends, trail continues north in drainage, do not turn right or left.

7.4 The trail splits. Continue upstream in the drainage closest to the base of Alto Relex (the ridge to your left) for the shortest route to the Telephone Canyon trailhead on Old Ore Road. The longer route, the one shown on topo maps, turns right, away from Alto Relex and into a drainage to the east.

9.4 The shortest route joins the Telephone Canyon Trail near top of a pass. Turn left to reach trailhead on Old Ore Road.

9.8 The longer route joins Telephone Canyon Trail in an arroyo. Turn left onto Telephone Canyon Trail to reach trailhead on Old Ore Road.

If you continue on to the Old Ore Road:

10.9 Telephone Canyon trailhead on Old Ore Road via the shorter route.

12.8 Telephone Canyon trailhead on Old Ore Road via the longer route.

36 Ernst Tinaja

General description: A day hike up a dry wash to Ernst Tinaja, a natural rock water hole.
Distance: 0.5 mile one way.
Approximate hiking time: 30 minutes.

Difficulty: Easy.
Traffic: Moderate.
Trail surface: Sand, gravel, and cobbles of dry desert wash.
Topo map: Roys Peak.

Finding the trailhead: The trail begins at the end of the 0.5-mile Ernst Tinaja Spur Road, about 4.5 miles from the southern end of Old Ore Road. Old Ore Road turns off of the north side of the road to Rio Grande Village about 18 miles from Panther Junction. Parking for the trailhead is available at the turnaround at the end of the spur road, just past the primitive campsite. Old Ore Road and the Ernst Tinaja Spur are primitive dirt roads that usually require high clearance and sometimes four-wheel drive. You should check road conditions with a park ranger before beginning your trip.

The Hike

Ernst Tinaja is reached by simply walking up the dry wash for about 0.5 mile. The word tinaja (pronounced ti-NA-ha) is Spanish for "large earthen jar," and refers to a basin-shaped water hole, usually carved into bedrock by natural erosion. These water holes are important sources of water in the canyons and rocky terrain of the Chihuahuan Desert. Insects, birds, snakes, frogs, deer, mountain lions, bears, and other creatures all depend on water sources like Ernst Tinaja for survival. Because of that, be careful never to contaminate any water source with soap, sunscreen, or other pollutants.

The water hole creates a welcome oasis, hidden away in the dry, inhospitable Dead Horse Mountains. It is hot in summer, but the canyon walls provide some shade. The permanent supply of water supports a tiny, isolated community of plants and animals, where small-scale, life-and-death struggles are played out every day. A small spring may add water to the tinaja because it never seems to dry up. When the water level gets low, animals sometimes drown because they are unable to climb back out.

The canyon containing Ernst Tinaja cuts through Cuesta Carlota, the western edge of the Dead Horse Mountains. As you wander up the wash, notice the tilted layers of bedrock emerging from the blanket of stream gravel. The canyon walls

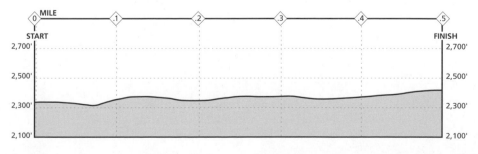

expose tilted and folded rock layers, with intricate patterns of red, orange, purple, and gray. Because of the huge faults and uplifts that created these mountains, the originally flat-lying beds now slope steeply to the west.

Unlike the Chisos Mountains, which were formed by the intrusion of molten igneous rock, the Dead Horse and Sierra del Carmen ranges are enormous blocks of limestone that were uplifted along faults. The Mesa de Anguila on the western side of the park was formed by a similar uplift, leaving the majority of the park in a sunken block of Earth's crust between two raised mountain ranges.

As you continue up the wash, you are walking back in geologic time toward older and older strata. Watch how the rock beds change as you approach the tinaja, becoming thinner and changing from relatively pure whitish limestone to colorful shale and limestone. The fossils of large clams and other marine creatures show that these beds were originally deposited on the ocean floor about 90 million years ago, during the Cretaceous period. Geologists have named these rocks the Boquillas Formation. This lowermost part of the Boquillas Formation is further distinguished as the Ernst Member, named after Ernst Tinaja.

At the tinaja, another rock formation, the Buda Limestone, is exposed. Ernst Tinaja is a large depression carved by erosion into the top of the Buda Limestone. This grayish white rock is composed of thick, massive beds of limestone, in sharp contrast with the thin, colorful beds of the overlying Boquillas Formation. This dramatic change in rock strata indicates a gap in the geologic record called an unconformity. The unconformity indicates a period of erosion or non-deposition of sediments that may have lasted for millions of years. During this time conditions changed in the ancient sea, changing the ways in which the rock layers were deposited and explaining the different appearance of the two rock formations.

As the thin clay-rich beds of the Boquillas Formation were deposited on the uneven, eroded surface of the Buda Limestone, they may have slipped and slumped occasionally. This is probably what caused the intricate folds you see near the tinaja.

You may continue up the canyon above the tinaja for a limited distance before the way is blocked by huge boulders and steep slickrock. If rain threatens, do not stay in the canyon. Flash floods occasionally sweep down, washing away everything in their path. If you wish to cross to the eastern side of Cuesta Carlota, hike the abandoned road that intersects the Old Ore Road about 1 mile south of the Ernst Tinaja Spur Road.

Miles and Directions

0.0   Trailhead at end of Ernst Tinaja Spur Road.

0.1   Rock outcrops (Boquillas Formation) in dry wash.

0.5   Ernst Tinaja.

◀ *Ernst Tinaja usually holds a deep pool of water.*

Ernst Tinaja

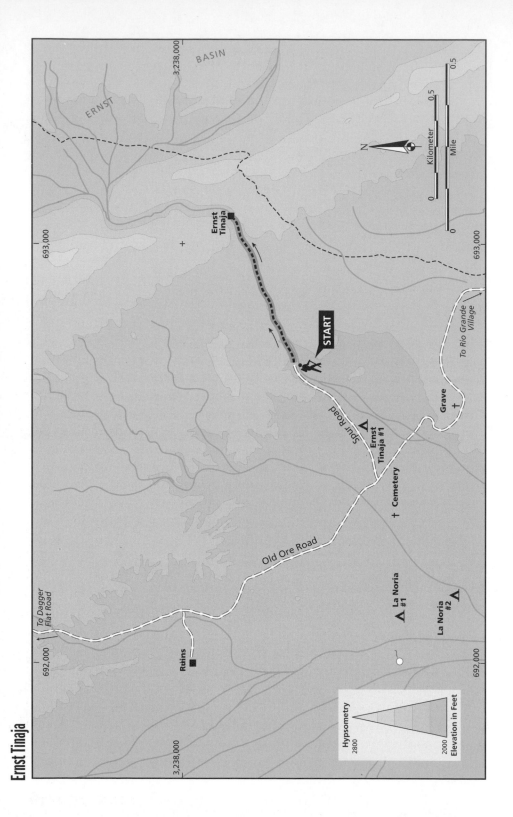

ERNST BASIN

3,238,000

693,000

Ernst Tinaja

START

Spur Road

Ernst Tinaja #1

Grave

To Rio Grande Village

Cemetery

Old Ore Road

La Noria #1

La Noria #2

Ruins

To Dagger Flat Road

692,000

3,238,000

693,000

692,000

N

Kilometer

Mile

0   0.5   0.5

Hypsometry

2800

2000

Elevation in Feet

37 Chihuahuan Desert Nature Trail

General description: A nearly level and well-marked day hike through Chihuahuan Desert terrain by a small oasis.
Distance: 0.5 mile loop.
Approximate hiking time: 30 minutes.

Difficulty: Easy. Not paved, but barrier-free with assistance.
Traffic: Heavy.
Trail surface: Dirt path.
Topo map: Panther Junction.

Finding the trailhead: The trail is located at Dugout Wells at the end of a short gravel spur road 6 miles southeast of Panther Junction on the road to Rio Grande Village. The trail begins across the gravel road from the picnic tables and is marked by a wooden sign.

The Dugout Wells windmill is silhouetted against the Sierra del Carmen of Mexico.

Chihuahuan Desert Nature Trail

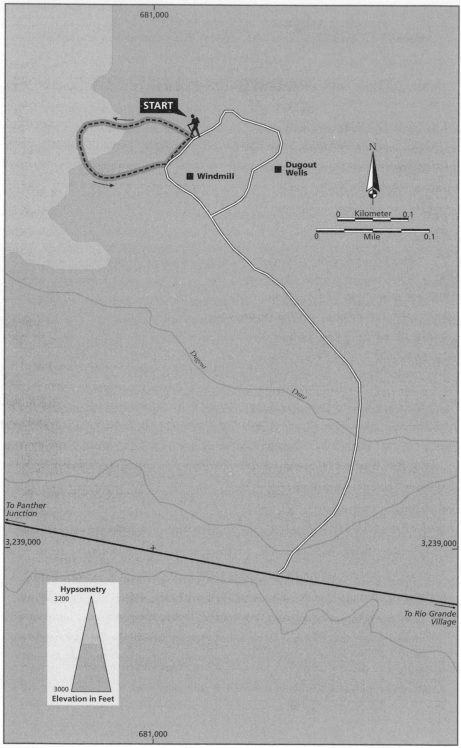

The Hike

By strolling this easy trail, you will find many interpretive signs that explain desert ecology. It winds through typical Chihuahuan Desert vegetation, offering a taste of the middle elevation desert plant communities that cover so much of Big Bend National Park. Due to its elevation and lack of shade, this trail can be extremely hot from late spring through early fall. Shady cottonwoods around the picnic tables provide relief from the desert sun on hot days. Water seeping to the surface feeds a small oasis here. During mild weather you can often see lizards, desert cottontail rabbits, and numerous birds along the path. Look for rodent tunnels along the trail and under plants.

The Avery family settled here in 1904 because of the permanent water source. They may have dug the well at the spring, which some people claim gives the location its name. Others believe Dugout Wells was named for the dugout house or jacal found here when the Green family purchased the land in 1917. Look for the remains of a dugout house, sections of barbed wire fence, and non-native fruit trees as you walk the trail. Feel free to examine any artifacts you find but please leave them where you find them for future visitors to see.

Big Bend residents once considered Dugout Wells the social and cultural center of the area. One of four elementary schools in the lower Big Bend was located here. Students and teachers walked miles from neighboring ranches and farms to come to school. Travelers often stopped to enjoy the shade, water their stock, and exchange news with local people. In 1938 the Greens sold the Dugout Wells property to the state of Texas, which donated it to the federal government for inclusion in Big Bend National Park.

Miles and Directions

0.0 Trailhead at Dugout Wells.
0.5 End of loop at trailhead.

38 Slickrock Canyon

General description: A cross-country day hike to a scenic canyon near the park's north boundary.

Distance: 4 miles one way.

Approximate hiking time: 2 hours.

Difficulty: Moderate, because of some route-finding.

Traffic: Light.

Trail surface: Dirt path.

Topo maps: Tule Mountain, The Basin.

Finding the trailhead: Drive west from park headquarters at Panther Junction toward Study Butte and the west park entrance. Just past mile marker 11, cross a bridge over Oak Creek. Beyond this, on the north side of the road, is a pullout. Park here and walk along the road back to the bridge, rather than parking on the shoulder. Climb down into the Oak Creek wash here and head downstream to the north.

The Hike

Slickrock Canyon is a small but scenic canyon located near the northern boundary of the park, just north of the Santa Elena Junction where the Ross Maxwell Scenic Drive turns off of the Panther Junction-Study Butte road. The walk is flat and easy, but there is no trail. The hike is a cross-country route that follows two washes to the canyon. You will be walking in sandy and gravelly wash conditions for the entire trip.

Begin walking downstream in Oak Creek from the road. The walk is almost level; although you are hiking downstream, the rate of fall is very gentle. There is no shade along the unmarked route. This can be a very hot hike in summer. Water can often be found along the route, but it is unreliable and often of poor quality. Plan to carry all that you need.

Slickrock Canyon is on the Tule Mountain topographic map. It is helpful to have this map to locate the correct wash to follow from the Oak Creek wash. The first mile of the route in Oak Creek north of the road is found on the Basin map; although it is helpful to have this map, it is not as vital as the Tule Mountain map.

Follow Oak Creek northwest by walking in the creekbed for about 2.5 miles. The walking is almost flat, but the area is exposed to both sun and wind. You will encounter typical desert wash vegetation along the way; skeleton-leaf goldeneye, desert willow, baccharis, mesquite, and creosote bush abound. You will see evidence of animals that use this wash as a travel route, too. Tracks and scat of coyote, fox, and javelina are common.

After hiking 1.5 miles or so, you will be able to see Slickrock Canyon some distance across desert flats to your right. During some times of the year, you may find water in Oak Creek in this area. Continue hiking until the canyon is directly on your right. It may even seem as though you are going past the canyon, but keep following the Oak Creek wash. You will eventually meet a smaller wash coming in from your right, the northeast. Although it is tempting to shortcut across the flats

Slickrock Canyon

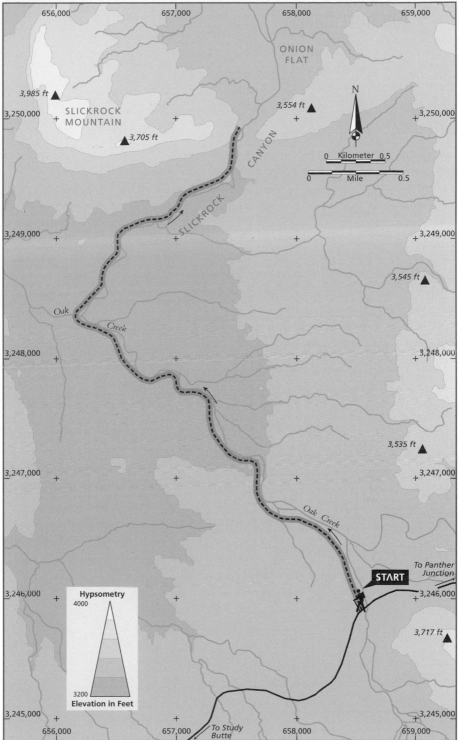

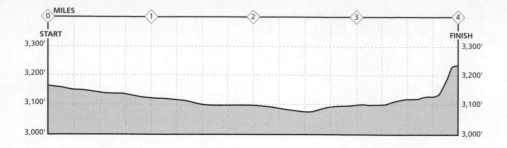

before you reach this wash, it will save you time and frustration if you wait until you reach the wash. Vegetation has grown thickly on the desert flats, making walking in the wash considerably easier. Follow this side wash until you reach the canyon in about 1.5 miles.

As you get within about 0.5 mile of Slickrock Canyon, look for a large pool of water that is present most of the time. This is a good place to look for tracks of javelina, ringtail, and mountain lion. Right before the canyon entrance notice the mortar holes in the bedrock of the creek, evidence that this area was used, at least seasonally, by prehistoric people.

Water has carved Slickrock Canyon deep into the side of Slickrock Mountain. You can walk a short distance through the canyon to Onion Flat, just north of the canyon. Immediately after passing through the canyon, you can explore the remains of an old windmill, earthen tank, and water tank just to the left of the wash. There is also an old well in this area, so be careful where you walk. The easiest way to return to the trailhead is by retracing your steps.

Miles and Directions

0.0 Trailhead where Oak Creek crosses road.

2.5 Enter side wash on right from Oak Creek wash.

4.0 Slickrock Canyon.

39 Grapevine Hills

General description: A day hike into the jumbled boulder pile of the Grapevine Hills, ending at a stone window.

Distance: 1 mile one way.

Approximate hiking time: 30 minutes.

Difficulty: Easy.

Traffic: Moderate.

Trail surface: Dirt path and sand, gravel, and cobbles of desert wash.

Topo map: Grapevine Hills.

Finding the trailhead: Drive west from Panther Junction headquarters about 3 miles on the road to Study Butte. Just after passing the Basin turnoff on the left, look for the sign for the Grapevine Hills road on the right. Follow the Grapevine Hills road for about 6.5 miles; the trailhead will be on the right. It is a small gravel parking area with an exhibit about the Grapevine Hills. Parking at this trailhead is limited. If you have a large vehicle, it is possible that you may not find adequate space, especially during busy times such as college spring break or Thanksgiving.

This is a gravel road; generally all vehicles except those with very low clearance can drive it. However, if you have a low-clearance car, you will have to drive carefully for the last 2 or 3 miles to avoid scraping the underside of your car on rocks. You may want to check on road conditions at a park visitor center before your trip.

The Hike

The Grapevine Hills Trail is a relatively easy 1-mile walk, most of it on relatively flat terrain. You will be walking in and out of a sandy wash for the first 0.75 mile with a gradual rise in elevation. For the last 0.25 mile, the trail becomes more strenuous as it climbs up a short but steep rocky slope before ending at a large balanced rock perched overhead between two rock pinnacles that creates a stone arch.

Although there are occasional bits of shade in the lee of boulders and pinnacles, this is usually a hot hike from April through September. If you hike during the hot season, be sure to get an early start. There is no water on the trail, so carry plenty any time of year.

The obvious trail heads south-southeast into the small canyon leading out of the back side of the parking area. The first 0.75 mile of the trail follows a desert wash upstream through the canyon and winds in and out of the sandy streambed. Although there are several branches of the wash (it is called a braided channel), do not worry about following the wrong branch. The branches split and then rejoin later. Footprints of hikers before you typically lead up several of the branches. The soft sand of the wash gets a little tiring for walking, but the route is easy otherwise.

The wash is lined with typical desert vegetation. In addition to creosote bush, cenizo, skeleton-leaf goldeneye, and acacias, you will also see guayacan and persimmon in abundance. The wash is bounded by the scenic terrain of the Grapevine Hills; eroded rocks tower over you on either side of the canyon as you walk along.

The Grapevine Hills Trail ends at a stone window.

The Grapevine Hills formed when a mass of granitic rock weathered and eroded into unusual shapes. The rocks are igneous in origin and were created when molten rock intruded into overlying sedimentary rock. The magma cooled and hardened into a large dome-shaped body called a laccolith. Eventually erosion stripped away the softer overlying sedimentary rock and exposed the granite that we see today. Most of the giant granite boulders in the area were once rectangular and blocky, but as water seeped into fractures in the rock, the corners eroded more quickly than the sides, producing rounded shapes. This is called spheroidal weathering, and is much in evidence all along the trail.

The Grapevine Hills granite is composed of a mixture of minerals, including quartz, feldspars, and mica. The weaker minerals erode faster creating a rough surface on exposed rocks. Shallow pits are often formed where rainwater pools on the rock rather than running off. Chemical reactions cause some of the minerals in the rock to slowly dissolve, creating a pit on the rock surface. Notice the wide variety of rock shapes as you hike the trail.

Grapevine Hills

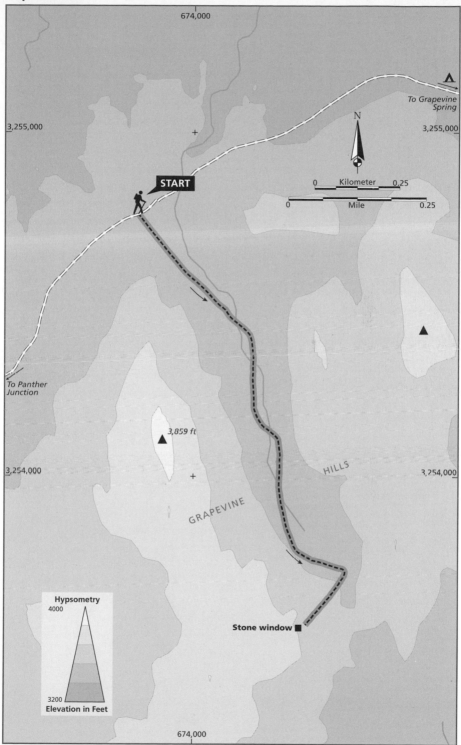

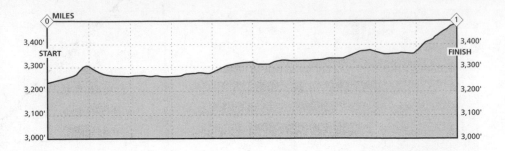

At the upper end of the wash, the trail begins to climb steeply upward and out of the small canyon to a low saddle. At the saddle, the trail turns sharply right and follows the ridge upward to the right. The route here winds through rock formations and is a bit confusing. Look for several small signs and metal fence posts to help guide you. It is only 100 yards or so to the arch at the end of the trail, but it is a steep climb among the rocks. You may need to use both hands and feet at some spots. Once at the balanced rock window, the view opens up toward the south and southeast; the most prominent feature is Nugent Mountain, about 10 miles away. The trail ends here; to return to the parking area, retrace your steps.

Miles and Directions

0.0 Trailhead on the Grapevine Hills road.

0.75 Trail climbs out of wash to a saddle.

1.0 Trail ends at stone window.

40 Dog Canyon

General description: A day hike across desert flats on the north side of the park to Dog Canyon, a deep cut through the Dead Horse Mountains.

Distance: 2.5 miles one way.

Approximate hiking time: 1.5 to 2 hours.

Difficulty: Easy, b̶̶̶̶ est route-finding.

Traffic: Light.

Trail surface: Di̶r̶̶̶̶

Topo maps: Bon̶̶̶̶

Finding the trailhead: The hike begins at the Dog Canyon Exhibit at a roadside pullout on the east side of the road about 3.5 miles south of the Persimmon Gap Visitor Center (or about 24 miles north of Panther Junction on the road to Marathon). The pullout is about 0.25 mile north of the bridge over Bone Spring Draw.

The Hike

There is no formal trail to Dog Canyon; however, it is an easy route to follow. The walk to the canyon can be traversed via one of two routes—by line of sight along a fairly well-worn social path across the desert flats or by entering Bone Spring/Nine Point Draw and following the dry arroyo downstream. This description traces the line of sight route across the desert.

This route can be traveled any season of the year. However, if you are hiking between mid-April and the end of September, this can be a very hot walk. There is no shade until you get to Dog Canyon and no water. During the hot time of year, plan this walk during early morning hours.

Even without a formal trail, this route is easy to follow because the destination, Dog Canyon, is easily visible for the entire hike. From the roadside pullout, Dog Canyon appears as a vertical gash slicing through the mountains about 2.5 miles east. To the north of Dog Canyon, the mountains are called the Santiago Mountains, to the south the Dead Horse Mountains. Both are part of a long chain of mountains stretching from near Alpine to deep into Mexico. In Mexico, the range is called the Sierra del Carmen.

From the parking lot, the path leads onto the desert flats. Although this is not a maintained trail, it is so well traveled that it is easily followed. If you stray from the path, just follow your eyes; Dog Canyon is always in sight.

The limestone Santiago and Dead Horse Mountains roughly mark the eastern boundary of Big Bend National Park. Limestones of the Santa Elena Formation form the cliff faces along the ridgetops while other geologic layers, prone to faster erosion, lie below. As these lower layers of rock weather away, the massive upper layers of Santa Elena Limestone are undercut and eventually collapse. A prominent scar, visible just north of Dog Canyon, formed from a thundering landslide in 1987. To highlight how distances can be deceiving in the desert, guess how large the boulders are within the debris pile. One of the huge rocks would fill your average-size kitchen.

About 0.25 mile into the hike, look for what appears to be a sidewalk to nowhere running north-south across the path. The pavement is what remains of an early road built decades ago. Also in this area are some small hills to the north and south that seem to contain concentric rings outlining their contours. Thin beds of Boquillas Limestone make up these hills and give them their appearance.

A field guide to Texas grasses is particularly valuable on this hike. At least a dozen species maintain a tenuous foothold in this stretch of desert flats. Although sparse, the diversity of grass species enduring in this hot, dry environment seems remarkable. However, if you study reports from early explorers or diaries from the first homesteaders, you read of an environment far different from what we see today. Their descriptions report a "sea of grass" in much of what today are mostly desert scrublands or bare patches of soil. Through overgrazing and decades of drought, the grasses disappeared. As the grasses were grazed off, fragile desert top-soils eroded away during heavy rains and desert shrubs invaded. The land lost its water-holding capability and water tables fell. Fire prevention and changes in rodent populations exacerbated the situation. In only a few decades, mankind greatly changed the land at Big Bend. Even with creation of the park sixty years ago, the land has only partly recovered.

Typical of the Chihuahuan Desert, cacti abound on these flats. A hike during late winter or spring would be the best time to catch prickly pear, pitaya, tasajillo, and dog cactus in bloom. Traveling in February, you might locate a mariposa cactus, one of the earliest cacti to flower, in full bloom. Later in the season, after any rainstorm, look for the beautiful pink flowers of eagle-claw cacti. About two-thirds of the way to Dog Canyon, you will pass a population of Torrey yucca. Like most of the other plant species along this route, the yuccas bloom around March.

Except during early morning or evening you probably will not see any animals. However, if you look carefully, their signs are all around. Listen for sparrows and thrashers rustling in the desert scrub and the call of the cactus wren. Mammals use the trail so keep an eye open for javelina and mule deer tracks. There are many bur-rows and holes tunneled into the desert floor that belong to creatures like badgers, ground squirrels, and tarantulas. The call of a coyote is commonplace throughout this uninhabited corner of the park, particularly early or late in the day. Animal scat lit-ters the terrain, obvious signs that wildlife does indeed survive in this harsh area.

About 0.5 mile from the canyon, the route drops down into Nine Point Draw. Dry most of the year, the arroyo can carry a raging flood after a thunderstorm. Nine Point Draw and its tributaries, such as Bone Spring Draw, provide drainage for much of this part of the park and can easily fill bank to bank with a danger-ous, muddy torrent.

◀ *A hiker walks through Dog Canyon.*

Dog Canyon; Devil's Den

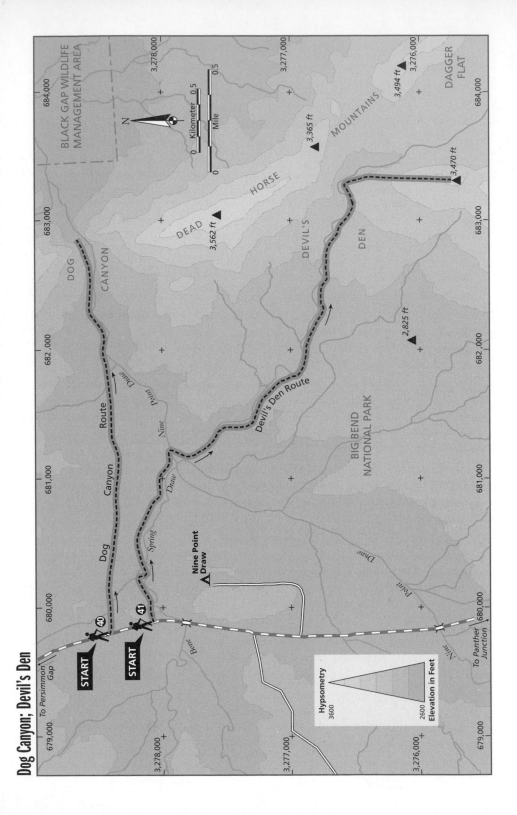

Follow the arroyo downstream and it will take you directly into Dog Canyon. Notice the vegetation paralleling the walls of Nine Point Draw. Although you will probably not encounter any surface water, precious reserves of moisture usually do exist within desert arroyos. Near these drainages, water becomes trapped from rainstorms and stored under the surface. Even though the amounts are sometimes small, the water reserves are nonetheless enough to create extraordinary changes in the desert habitat. Take note how this particular drainage is thickly lined with desert willow, Texas persimmon, Mexican buckeye, and other shrubs and small trees that could never survive in the more arid areas only 100 feet away from the arroyo.

As you enter Dog Canyon, the arroyo walls quickly gain height and change from gravel alluvium to massive limestone layers. In places the gorge contains small caves that give the appearance of limestone dissolving away. In other areas, the old grayish rock surface has eroded off, uncovering a fresh interior that contributes an orange color to the cliff faces.

The geologic highlight of Dog Canyon is its south wall, just before you exit the far end. There, the once horizontal layers of rock have been uplifted and now lie in a slightly curved vertical formation. Erosion has chiseled away some of the layers faster than others, creating an unusual appearance.

To hike back, retrace your steps but watch for where the trail leaves Nine Point Draw on the north side and heads back across the desert flats. If you miss the spot, you can follow the drainage back to the road but it will add some distance to the hike. If you do follow the draw back to the highway, be sure to turn right at the road and follow it back north to the trailhead. Before you depart for the return trek, however, take a moment to relax in the cool confines of this short canyon.

Miles and Directions

0.0 Trailhead at Dog Canyon Exhibit.

2.5 Dog Canyon.

41 Devil's Den

General description: A cross-country day hike to the narrow chasm of Devil's Den.
Distance: 3.25 miles one way.
Approximate hiking time: 1.5 to 2 hours.

Difficulty: Moderate, due to lack of any maintained trail and required route-finding.
Traffic: Very light.
Trail surface: Dirt path and cross-country.
Topo maps: Bone Spring, Dagger Flat.

Finding the trailhead: This hike begins near the bridge crossing Bone Spring Draw, about 3.5 miles south of the Persimmon Gap Visitor Center (or about 24 miles north of Panther Junction on the road to Marathon). Just north of the bridge, an abandoned gravel road goes east from the main park road. Park at this junction, but do not block the gate on the old road.

The Hike

The route follows several arroyos, or dry washes, up the south rim of Devil's Den Canyon, and ends high atop the back side of this narrow canyon. The views from this ridge provide a seldom-seen look into a hidden valley within the Dead Horse Mountains—the true Dagger Flat. As with all primitive routes at Big Bend, you need a topographic map and good hiking skills for Devil's Den.

This route can be traveled any season of the year. However, if you are hiking between mid-April and the end of September, this hike can be very hot. During that time of year, avoid extreme afternoon temperatures by walking during early morning hours. Wear long pants to protect your legs on this cross-country route. There is no water, so carry plenty. Avoid the arroyos during thunderstorms; they can flood quickly, and afterward the drainages may become too muddy to hike. Unless you have good rock-climbing skills, you should not attempt to hike through Devil's Den itself since it contains large boulders, potholes, and pour-offs that block the route. Be cautious where the route follows the sheer walls of the canyon rim.

Looking east toward the mountains from the road, Dog Canyon is a very prominent deep canyon cutting through the northern saddle of a dome-like mountain. Devil's Den is a less-obvious canyon cutting through the southern saddle of this domed mountain. It appears as a dark and narrow slit zigzagging its way up the hillside to a saddle. This route's destination is the top of the saddle, where Devil's Den begins in Dagger Flat. Although the approach from this western flank gradually slopes upward to the top of the ridge, the eastern side (hidden from view from the trailhead) forms cliffs rising several hundred feet above the Dagger Flat valley.

From your vehicle, drop into Bone Spring Draw, the arroyo immediately east of the road, and follow it downstream toward the mountains. In about 0.25 mile, the ruins of an old concrete bridge span the drainage. The bridge and pavement on the

Devil's Den forms a deep, narrow canyon. ▶

desert surface are what remain of an early road built decades ago. In this first section of the route, Bone Spring Draw meanders gently through gravelly alluvium with periodic outcrops of whitish limestone layers.

The highlight along this stretch is the diversity of shrubs eking out an existence in this section of the Chihuahuan Desert. Although dry for most of the year, arroyos like Bone Spring Draw capture and store moisture during the summer thunderstorm season. Environmental conditions along the desert arroyos are changed only slightly, but enough to favor more growth than would be expected in such a harsh environment. Dozens of species of shrubs line the route, including honey mesquite, desert willow, Texas persimmon, huisache, and catclaw acacia.

In just less than a mile, Bone Spring Draw empties into a much larger drainage, Nine Point Draw. The intersection is quite obvious, with Nine Point Draw converging from the right and slightly above the arroyo you are in. The meeting of these two drainages creates a large gravel and sand bar about 60 feet wide. Carefully note the surrounding features, for you will want to make sure you re-enter Bone Spring Draw on the return trip.

The gravel bar makes a sweeping arc to the left. Just about 100 yards downstream from this intersection, look for the first drainage cutting off to the right at a sharp angle—it is the arroyo that leads to Devil's Den. This unnamed drainage is much narrower than Bone Spring and Nine Point Draws, and sometimes the path is restricted by thorny brush encroaching into the arroyo. Follow this drainage as it slowly climbs upstream and meanders southeast.

After traveling about a mile in this arroyo, another impressive plant species makes its appearance—the giant dagger yucca. A few specimens of this huge yucca dot the upper terraces of the drainage like pioneers slowly progressing downward from the core population in Dagger Flat.

Just after the first giant dagger yuccas, the low gravel banks of the drainage give way to higher rocky walls. These orange-mottled layers are members of the Boquillas Formation and add a welcome splash of color to the monotonous tones of the area. The drainage soon makes a sharp curve to the left and enters a rock grotto. Look carefully and you will find a well-camouflaged tinaja, or rock water hole, next to a small natural bridge.

Within the next 0.25 mile upstream from the grotto, large boulders begin to litter the drainage. Here the route disappears. Ahead, the arroyo walls become higher and higher. Watch the right bank for a break in the vegetation, and when one appears, work your way out of the drainage. Once you climb out, look for a faint path. As you follow the rim of Devil's Den Canyon upstream, the trail eventually appears and parallels the canyon along the south rim.

The route gradually ascends the hillside as it parallels Devil's Den Canyon and provides continually changing views into the narrow chasm. At the top of a saddle, where Devil's Den reaches its deepest point, the canyon walls abruptly end and the drainage opens up into a broad valley, Dagger Flat.

If you expend a little extra effort, you can continue for a half mile or so south along the valley rim to an obvious outcrop creating a high point above the valley. From this promontory, the view southeast provides for an extraordinary sight—the far end of the valley below contains a forest of giant dagger yuccas. With binoculars, the high number and density of yuccas in this valley, the real Dagger Flat, becomes clear. Although the views of Devil's Den and the hidden Dagger Flat are impressive, few people ever venture here. The accompanying guidebook map shows this hiking route, although there are others, as described below.

It is possible to hike through the canyon, but you must have good rock-climbing skills. It requires climbing over numerous dropoffs up to 6 feet high, sometimes dropping into waist-deep pools of water. The rock itself is very smooth and offers few handholds. Since these slick pour-offs are easier to climb down than up, it is possible to become trapped between tricky climbs above and below you. You will be climbing down the pour-offs by hiking the canyon from east to west, and up the pour-offs by hiking from west to east.

This description assumes that you hike up the rim and descend through the canyon bottom. At the top of the saddle described earlier, where the canyon walls abruptly end and the drainage opens up into Dagger Flat, angle toward the right at the top of this ridge to find a notch that will allow you to hike down the east side of the hill into a creekbed that leads left into Devil's Den.

The dropoffs and seasonal pools of water appear immediately within the upper entrance of Devil's Den, along with the remains of a high dam. The route through the canyon takes you over many slick pour-offs, sometimes into pools of water, as well as over and around many large boulders. Once you have committed to hiking down a few of these pour-offs, you may not be able to climb back up them. As you follow the winding canyon westward, the canyon walls will eventually become lower, until you find yourself again at the base of the canyon.

A second possible route begins at the Dog Canyon trailhead a short distance north along the highway from the trailhead described above. From the parking area, hike toward Dog Canyon, then turn south and drop into Bone Spring Draw, the large arroyo heading toward the east used by the main route above. From that point, follow the same directions as above.

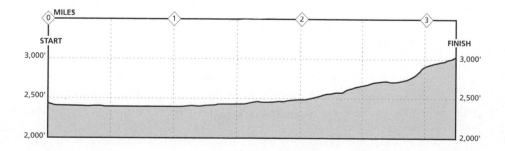

Another route involves parking along the dirt spur road that leads off the high-way near mile marker 22 to the Nine Point Draw backcountry campsite. From here, just hike cross-country toward the dark, jagged slit of Devil's Den visible in the mountain to the east. Once you reach the canyon, follow the directions above.

A third and longer route to Devil's Den also begins at the Dog Canyon trailhead. A topographic map and good route-finding and map-reading skills are particularly important for this variation. Follow the Dog Canyon Trail into and through Dog Canyon. Once you have gone through the canyon, turn right (south) and hike cross-country along the base of the mountains on your right. By using your map and watching carefully, locate a pass in the mountains after about 1.5 miles. Climb up and over the pass into the north end of Dagger Flat, the broad valley mentioned above that drains into Devil's Den.

Miles and Directions

0.0 Trailhead on road.

0.25 Old bridge.

0.9 Bone Spring Draw joins Nine Point Draw.

2.0 Bottom of Devil's Den Canyon.

2.75 Top of Devil's Den.

3.25 High point above Dagger Flat.

42 Estufa Canyon/Banta Shut-in

General description: A strenuous day hike or backpack to the Banta Shut-in on Tornillo Creek.

Distance: 7.5 miles one way.

Approximate hiking time: 4 to 5 hours.

Difficulty: Strenuous.

Traffic: Very light.

Trail surface: Dirt path and sand, gravel, and cobbles of dry desert wash.

Topo maps: Panther Junction, Roys Peak.

Finding the trailhead: Drive 2 miles east of Panther Junction toward Rio Grande Village and turn left, or east, on the gravel K-Bar Road, driving to where it ends at a primitive campsite. Be sure that you do not park in the campsite. The trail begins at the east side of K-Bar primitive campsite 2 (marked with a signpost reading KB-2) and follows an old roadway toward the east.

The Hike

The Estufa Canyon/Banta Shut-in hike can be a long, strenuous day hike, but is better done as an overnight backpacking trip. Water is often available at the shut-in, but is not always reliable. You should ask at the nearby Panther Junction Visitor Center about the status of water sources on the route before beginning the hike. Without clear confirmation of water availability, plan on carrying all your water.

Because of frequent daytime highs of more than 100 degrees Fahrenheit on this trail during the summer, this hike should be considered a late fall to early spring hike. The canyon walls at the Banta Shut-in and in places along Estufa Canyon provide some welcome shade at various times of day on this hike. Remember not to camp in a dry wash like Estufa Canyon because of the danger of flash floods, especially during the summer and early fall rainy season.

The route starts down the old road leading east from the primitive campsite. After about 0.5 mile, the route branches off to the north and becomes a true hiking trail marked with rock cairns. The route continues northeast, winding through side washes, reaching Estufa Canyon after about 1.75 miles. On the north wall of the canyon is evidence of a wildfire that burned 3,774 acres of the park in July 1994. This was the largest fire in Big Bend National Park history up to this time.

Starting here at a large rock cairn, the route turns right, downstream, and is marked with rock cairns throughout Estufa Canyon. If the cairns are missing from floods or other causes, don't worry, just follow the wash downstream. Three miles of travel down the canyon brings you to some unusual rock formations along the canyon walls where erosion has been at work. The varied shapes of these formations, which continue for some distance, can be especially scenic right before dark, when the walls of the canyon seem to catch fire with the light of the setting sun. Perhaps the name of the canyon, Estufa, the Spanish word for stove, may have its origins in this phenomenon.

Estufa Canyon/Banta Shut-in

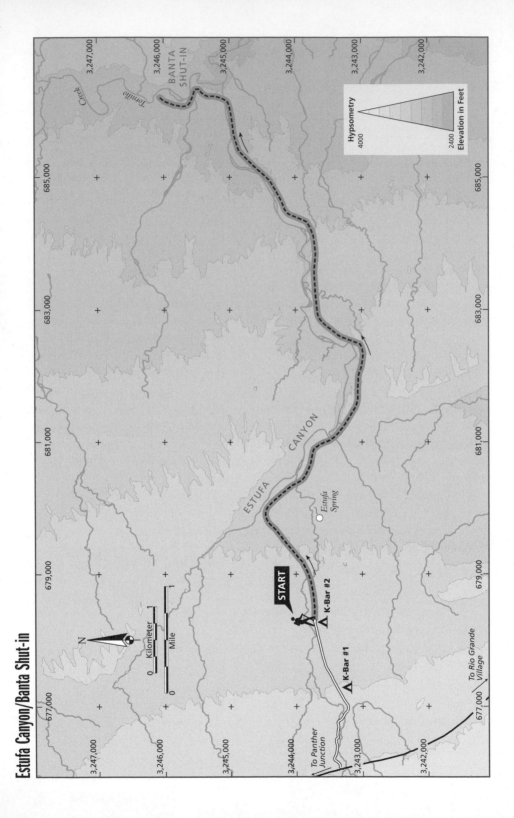

At about 7 miles, Estufa Canyon joins Tornillo Creek. Turn left and proceed northward up the creek. You may want to build some temporary rock cairns at the confluence to help find your way back up Estufa Canyon on your return. People sometimes get confused by the number of drainages that come together where Estufa Canyon flows into Tornillo Creek. The Spanish name tornillo translates to "screw," and refers to a species of mesquite tree that has screw-shaped bean pods. In the late 1800s and early 1900s, when settlers first arrived in the Big Bend region, there were so many tornillo mesquite trees lining this creek that they named it Tornillo. Today, the almost total absence of any kind of tree, including the mesquites, along the creek testifies to the impact that settlement, mining, and overgrazing had on the scarce wood resources of this Chihuahuan Desert region.

The final 0.5 mile of walking brings you to the Banta Shut-in, a narrow canyon of dark igneous rock, probably the most constricted section of Tornillo Creek. At the north end of the Banta Shut-in is an intermittent spring that can be quite beautiful when it is flowing. It can be difficult to walk through the shut-in without getting wet because of a large pool of water; it may be necessary to hike around the shut-in to travel upstream. Please remember that wildlife is completely dependent on natural water sources like these and that visitors should be careful not to contaminate them or camp too close.

Miles and Directions

0.0 Trailhead at K-Bar primitive campsite 2.

0.5 Trail leaves old roadway.

1.75 Trail reaches Estufa Canyon. Follow it downstream.

4.75 Rock formations in Estufa Canyon.

7.0 Estufa Canyon enters Tornillo Creek; turn left up Tornillo Creek.

7.5 Banta Shut-in.

43 Persimmon Gap Draw

General description: A day hike up Persimmon Gap Draw through some interesting geologic sites, including the park's oldest rocks.
Distance: 1 mile one way.
Approximate hiking time: 30 minutes.

Difficulty: Easy.
Traffic: Very light.
Trail surface: Dirt path.
Topo map: Persimmon Gap.

Finding the trailhead: The hike begins at the Persimmon Gap Visitor Center at the north end of the park.

The Hike

Big Bend National Park contains a variety of hidden treasures, those seldom-visited hideaways that contain unexpected sights. The hike up Persimmon Gap Draw is one of the least traveled at Big Bend, yet the rewards of walking it are worth the time and effort. It leads to fascinating geologic features, including the oldest exposed rocks in the park. Along the route you will encounter desert shrubs and many species of lizards. The hike ends with a pleasant view north of the park.

This route can be traveled any season of the year, but if you are hiking between April and October, plan this walk early in the day to avoid the heat. The route is easy overall, but does have one steep grade where it climbs around a pour-off and a short scramble up a 6-foot pile of boulders at a second pour-off.

Persimmon Peak rises against the sky to the east, directly across the road from the Persimmon Gap Visitor Center. Just north of it lies a smaller unnamed peak. The hike up Persimmon Gap Draw ends on a saddle between these two summits.

To start, walk across the road from the visitor center and go a short distance north along the road to where it crosses a dry wash. Drop down into the wash and follow it upstream to the east as it gently winds through Chihuahuan Desert terrain. Texas persimmon trees, with their smooth, light gray bark, thrive throughout this drainage; hence the name Persimmon Gap. Bring along two field guides: one to identify desert shrubs and one for lizards, common during the warm months of the year. Forget your geology guide—even experts struggle to decipher what has happened here.

The first 0.5 mile provides seasonal variety in plants and animals. Torrey yucca and prickly pear cactus blossom in the spring; wildflowers bloom after the summer rains. Eagle claw cacti bloom whenever it rains during warm months. With similar timing, clumps of blue-gray cenizo shrubs show off their pink or blue flowers after the first thunderstorms of June.

◀ *Prickly pear cacti thrive in the Persimmon Gap area.*

Persimmon Gap Draw

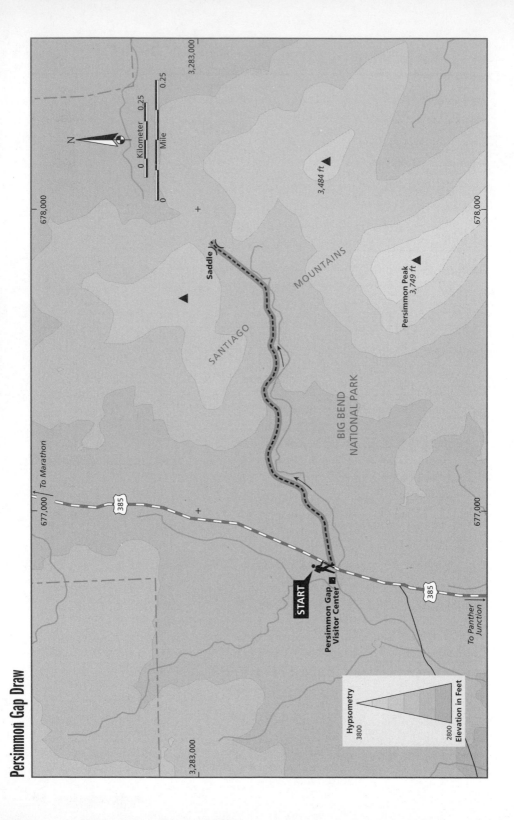

Halfway up the wash is a pour-off, a dry waterfall approximately 70 feet high. About 70 feet before it, an unmaintained path leads up around the right side of the obstacle. Make your way carefully up the gravelly path, the only steep part of the hike. When the path ends near the top of the pour-off, veer off onto the rocks to your right. At the top, make your way back into the wash and continue up the drainage.

About 100 feet beyond the pour-off is a splendid view of Persimmon Peak with its convoluted cliff face—particularly beautiful in the light of the setting sun. Geologists have names for the various rock layers: Glen Rose, San Vicente, Pen, and Aguja. These rocks, mostly limestones and sandstones, all date from the Cretaceous period. More interesting, however, are the older Paleozoic Tesnus, Maravillas, and Caballos Formations—the ancient rocks of Big Bend. As Persimmon Gap Draw begins to narrow, you get a close-up view of these three formations. The Tesnus Formation consists of sandstones and green cherts, the Maravillas Formation of gray to black limestones and black chert, and the Caballos Formation of predominantly white chert.

Continue in the main drainage and look for a small cave along the right side of the draw's steepening walls. Soon after, a hidden alcove also lies in the right bank. Beyond the alcove the wash gently meanders along. Every turn displays different twisted and folded geologic layers, each more fascinating than the previous ones.

The hike is about three-quarters complete when you come to the small second pour-off. Rock outcroppings here are composed of chalky white rock, the Caballos Formation, the oldest exposed rock in Big Bend National Park.

Scramble up the pour-off, watching your footing. Ahead, the shrinking drainage splits; stay in the left fork. Eventually it too divides into ever-smaller channels. At this point, leave the wash and work your way to the top of the small gap, or saddle, straight ahead. Carefully pick your way up the slope on broken rock layers and loose gravel.

The vantage point atop the saddle offers a view few people ever see. To the northeast, beyond the park, you see a vast stretch of Texas rangeland dotted with low mesas and buttes on the horizon. Behind you to the southwest, another view, somewhat restricted but equally impressive, showcases the Christmas Mountains 25 miles away.

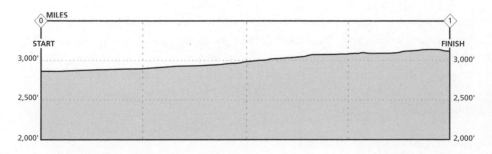

To hike back, retrace your route. On the way, pause for a moment at the dark rocks of the Maravillas Formation. In English, maravillas translates into "marvelous," an apt description for Persimmon Gap Draw.

Miles and Directions

0.0 Trailhead.

0.5 First pour-off.

1.0 Saddle below Persimmon Peak.

44 Mesa de Anguila

General description: A rough backpack to Tinaja Lujan on remote Mesa de Anguila. Many other hikes of various lengths and difficulties are also possible.
Distance: 7.5 miles one way.
Approximate hiking time: 3.5 to 4 hours.

Difficulty: Moderate to strenuous; requires good map-reading and route-finding skills.
Traffic: Very light.
Trail surface: Dirt path and cross-country.
Topo maps: Lajitas, Mesa de Anguila.

Finding the trailhead: The main trailhead is in the village of Lajitas immediately behind the Lajitas golf course. Ask at the Panther Junction Visitor Center for a sketch map of the trailhead location when you obtain your backcountry permit.

There are several other trails and routes onto Mesa de Anguila, all of them more difficult. You can hike onto the mesa on the east side from Terlingua Abaja; a primitive 3-mile trail leads from this campsite to Bruja Canyon. You then face a rough rock scramble and climb up the right side of the canyon wall. Two trails from the river also lead onto the mesa from Metates and Entrance Camps.

The Hike

Mesa de Anguila is one of the least visited areas of Big Bend National Park. It is part of a large uplift that extends across the Rio Grande deep into Mexico. In Texas the mesa is known as Mesa de Anguila; in Mexico it is called the Sierra Ponce. The deep cut of Santa Elena Canyon separates the two and marks the border.

The complex of trails on Mesa de Anguila offers numerous options for long or short hikes of varying difficulties. The lack of water, extreme summer temperatures, and a maze of trails make hiking here challenging. Mesa trails are rarely maintained, so expect abundant spiny vegetation and loose rocks. Wear long pants or gaiters for protection from vegetation on overgrown trails. Mesa de Anguila is usually very hot from early April well into October. Hikes on the mesa should be done during cooler times of year.

The Mesa de Anguila Trail climbs onto the mesa that forms the right-hand, or Texas, wall of Santa Elena Canyon.

Trails are often faint and unmarked. Look for rock cairns to help you find your way. A compass and topographic maps, along with skill in using them, are essential for hikes on the mesa. Many old trails are not shown on the maps. Hikers should gain experience on other park trails before coming to Mesa de Anguila.

Do not expect to find water on the mesa. During and after the rainy season, rock pools known as tinajas often hold water; however, these are unreliable throughout the year. The tinajas provide limited water for all the desert animals of the area, so hikers should carry as much of their own water in as possible. If you must take water from any natural source, purify it before drinking.

Many hikes are possible on Mesa de Anguila, both short and extensive. Even a short day hike from Lajitas onto the mesa provides spectacular views of other mesas and colorful rock outcrops around Lajitas and in Mexico. On the mesa itself you will see many small canyons, cliffs, and *mesitas*.

One possible route is described here. Start at the main Lajitas trailhead by the golf course. The trail climbs to a saddle on the top of the mesa to the southeast. The trail to the base of the saddle is vague, but it is easy to see where you need to go.

The route climbs from the Lajitas trailhead to the top of the saddle in about 1.5 miles. From the top, you have expansive views of the mesa, the Rio Grande, and mountains in Mexico. From the top of the saddle, hike about 4.5 miles southeast across the mesa top to Tinaja Blanca, a natural rock water hole tucked into a small

Mesa de Anguila

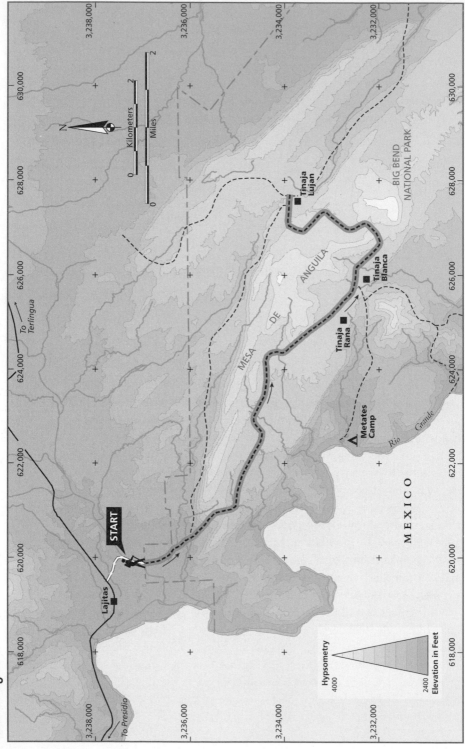

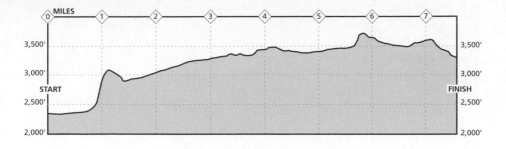

canyon. About 0.25 mile before this tinaja, you pass a junction with two trails turning right that lead down to the Rio Grande.

From Tinaja Blanca, it is about 1.5 miles east and then north to Tinaja Lujan, another water hole tucked into a small canyon. Three more routes meet near Tinaja Lujan. Several possibilities exist for extending your hike. A cairn-marked route leads down the large wash to the southeast toward Bruja Canyon and to the two largest tinajas on the mesa, Tinaja Grande and Tinaja Susan. The trail leading north from Tinaja Lujan winds its way to a large dam. You can make a loop hike back to the trailhead by following the northwestern route from Tinaja Lujan down a large canyon and back to the base of the mesa near Lajitas. Watch carefully for rock cairns to stay on the correct route.

Many other hikes are possible on the mesa. For instance, a base camp could be set up near Tinaja Blanca from which day hikes could be made. A long cross-country route would involve hiking southeast along the mesa top from Tinaja Blanca all the way to the rim of Santa Elena Canyon. Few people have seen the spectacular canyon from the rim. For other hikes, try descending the trails from near Tinaja Blanca to the river. Although mesa hikes require extra effort, the reward includes spectacular scenery and solitude.

Miles and Directions

0.0   Trailhead near Lajitas golf course.

1.5   Top of saddle.

5.75 Junction with two river trails.

6.0   Tinaja Blanca.

7.5   Tinaja Lujan.

Big Bend Ranch State Park

Adjacent to Big Bend National Park lies Big Bend Ranch State Park, an additional 250,000 acres of Chihuahuan Desert that invites exploration. The Texas Parks and Wildlife Department purchased the enormous tract in 1988, roughly doubling the size of the state park system. The state park fronts the Rio Grande west of Big Bend National Park between Lajitas and Presidio, and contains a rugged mix of desert mountains, canyons, and grasslands.

The Rio Grande flows through sheer-walled Colorado Canyon and forms the southern boundary of the state park. Texas Highway FM 170 follows the canyon, squeezed between mountains and the river, along one of the most spectacular routes in Texas. The reddish-brown, iron-stained walls of the canyon were carved by the Rio Grande through the Bofecillos Mountains of Texas and Sierra Rica of Mexico.

Like the national park, the entire state park lies within the Chihuahuan Desert. Except for small riparian areas along the Rio Grande and around springs and small permanent watercourses, desert vegetation dominates. Desert plants, such as lechuguilla, sotol, ocotillo, creosote, and numerous cactus species, are prolific. Much of the wildlife is found around water sources, where reeds, willows, salt cedar, cottonwood, and ash create a lush habitat. Commonly seen animals in the natural area include mule deer, javelina, and many species of lizards.

Humans arrived in the area at least 10,000 years ago, living in nomadic groups that hunted game and gathered edible fruits, nuts, berries, leaves, and roots. The earliest groups left few traces of their passing, other than projectile points and other stone tools. The remains of later groups left evidence of campsites, rock art, burials, and stone artifacts that dot Big Bend Ranch. The Spaniards arrived about 400 years ago, but made only sporadic efforts to control and settle the Big Bend area north of the Rio Grande. Comanche and Apache Indians limited settlement of the area until the late 1800s. Ranchers moved into the area after the Indian threat ended and silver and mercury mining began at nearby Shafter and Terlingua, respectively, in the late 1800s. Profitable ore eventually ran out in both mining districts; most operations ceased by the 1940s. Until tourism developed, ranching and farming along the Rio Grande floodplain remained the chief economic activities.

At Big Bend Ranch the Rio Grande has carved a deep chasm called Colorado Canyon.

Before starting a hike, stop in at the Barton Warnock Environmental Education Center in Lajitas. It has an extensive museum describing the human and natural history of the region, an elaborate desert garden, a bookstore, plus information and permits. Fort Leaton State Historical Park near Presidio also has information and permits, along with historical exhibits and a bookstore. Big Bend Ranch's administrative headquarters, across TX FM 170 from Fort Leaton, handles reservations for programs, camping, and lodging at Sauceda, in addition to permits and information. Hiking conditions are similar to those found in the neighboring national park, so prepare accordingly. As of this writing, three hiking trails have been developed in the state park and are described in the following pages. More trails are planned, so be sure to check in at the park visitor centers. Big Bend Ranch State Park is one of the crown jewels of the state park system. As more trails are developed, it will provide worthy competition to its better-known neighbor, Big Bend National Park.

For more information write to Big Bend Ranch State Park, P.O. Box 2319, Presidio, TX 79845 or call (432) 229–3416.

45 Closed Canyon

General description: A day hike into Closed Canyon, a narrow slot canyon at Big Bend Ranch State Park similar to those commonly found in Utah.

Distance: 0.7 mile one way.

Approximate hiking time: 30 minutes.

Difficulty: Easy.

Traffic: Moderate.

Trail surface: Dirt path.

Topo map: Redford SE.

Finding the trailhead: The Closed Canyon trailhead, marked as such by a trail sign and parking area on the south side of Texas Highway FM 170, lies 22 miles west of the Barton Warnock Environmental Education Center near Lajitas and 28 miles east of Fort Leaton State Historical Park near Presidio. Obtain a permit at the Warnock Center or Fort Leaton before hiking.

The Hike

Closed Canyon is a deep, narrow canyon cutting through Colorado Mesa to the Rio Grande. The trail follows the bottom of the canyon until a series of high pour-offs prevent further travel down canyon. The mouth of Closed Canyon is easily visible a short distance west of the trailhead. The trail starts at the TX FM 170 parking area by following an abandoned dirt road a short distance west to a dry creekbed that enters Closed Canyon. Follow the creekbed downstream into the canyon's entrance, where the gravel gives way to smooth, polished rock.

Closed Canyon gets its name from its narrow width; in some places the canyon can nearly be spanned by holding out your arms. It appears much like the narrow canyons of southern Utah, except that the rock is of different composition. It is often hiked even during hot desert summers because sunlight reaches the bottom for only a short time each day. Although the hike is hot in summer, plentiful shade created by the canyon walls make the hike bearable, especially early in the morning. The Spanish-speaking people of the area call it Cañon Oscuro, which translates to "Dark Canyon." The trail is suitable for families with sure-footed children, although children will have to be watched carefully at the pour-offs at the end of the hike.

Most of the canyon floor is smooth, water-worn rock, which can be very slippery when wet. It is necessary to crawl over some small boulders and scramble down short pour-offs. It is not possible to reach the Rio Grande, since after 0.7 mile the canyon bottom gives way to a series of high, vertical pour-offs. This is a good place to stop, rest, and listen to the subtle sounds of the desert resonating between the canyon's walls.

The canyon walls are made of a rock called welded tuff. Welded tuff is formed when a volcano erupts and spews out glowing, incandescent ash mixed with hot gases and liquids. As it settles to the ground, heat and pressure from succeeding layers "weld" the ash into rock. This formation is the Santana Tuff, ejected from a volcano in the Sierra Ricas in Mexico approximately 28 million years ago.

About 3 million years later, the region was racked by earthquakes in which large blocks of land were raised and lowered along faults. The broad valley at the entrance of Closed Canyon is called the Santana Bolson; it is a block of land bounded on the north and south by faults. The land between these faults dropped, forming a low area between Colorado Mesa and the Bofecillos Mountains to the north. The hiking trail crosses the southern fault at the entrance of Closed Canyon.

Before the Rio Grande cut through the Big Bend region, the Santana Bolson was filled with sediments deposited by erosion, completely covering Colorado Mesa. When the Rio Grande was born, a stream flowed across the top of Colorado Mesa into the river. As erosion cut into the land, both the river and the tributary stream continued to drop, carrying away the sediments and carving Closed Canyon and Colorado Canyon deeper and deeper. Oddly, the Rio Grande in Colorado Canyon is higher in elevation than some parts of the Santana Bolson.

Water is still cutting and polishing Closed Canyon. While hiking, be aware of the weather. Usually the canyon is dry, except for occasional pools sometimes left by previous floods. If a storm threatens or water begins to flow in the canyon, leave immediately. There is no safe place in Colorado Canyon in the event of a flash flood. Remember, even if it is not raining in the canyon itself, heavy rains on the upstream watershed can still flood the canyon.

Miles and Directions

0.0   Trailhead on TX FM 170.

0.7   End of trail where pour-offs prohibit further travel.

◀ *Water cut the deep, narrow slot of Closed Canyon.*

Closed Canyon

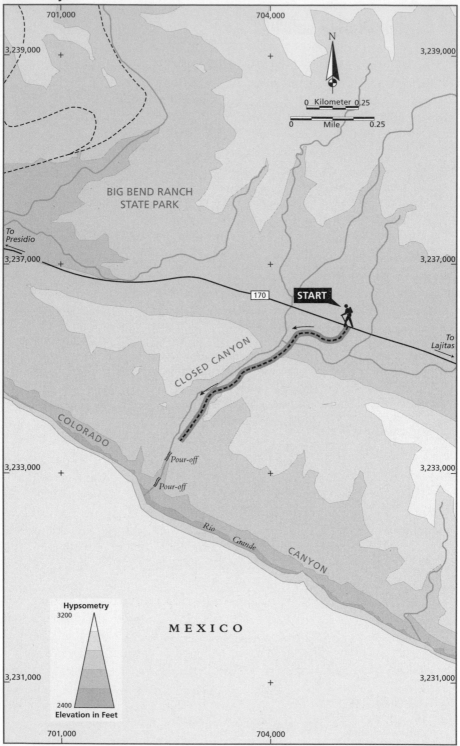

46 Rancherías Canyon

General description: A day hike up a spectacular, rugged canyon in Big Bend Ranch State Park.
Distance: 4.8 miles one way.
Approximate hiking time: 2.5 to 3 hours.

Difficulty: Moderately strenuous.
Traffic: Light.
Trail surface: Dirt path, gravel, and cobbles.
Topo maps: Redford SE, Agua Adentro Mountain.

Finding the trailhead: The Rancherías Canyon and the West Rancherías Loop trailhead are marked by a sign, W. RANCHERÍAS TRAILHEAD, on the north side of Texas Highway FM 170, 23 miles west from the Barton Warnock Environmental Education Center near Lajitas and 27 miles east of Fort Leaton State Historical Park near Presidio. Be sure to get a permit at the Barton Warnock Center or Fort Leaton first.

The Hike

Rancherías Canyon is a deep and wide canyon cutting through ancient lava flows in the southern Bofecillos Mountains.

The hike terminates at a box canyon at Rancherías Falls, a beautiful waterfall approximately 80 feet high. The trailhead starts at the parking area and follows a footpath along a dry creek drainage until it joins an old wagon road. After a short distance the road forks. Hikers wishing to hike Rancherías Canyon will take the right fork; the left fork is part of the Rancherías Loop Trail. The right fork drops down to the floor of Rancherías Canyon. From there the watercourse is followed upstream through the canyon all the way to the end at the box canyon. Rock cairns mark the way from the trailhead to the falls.

The word ranchería is a diminutive of the Spanish word rancho, or ranch. It was often used to describe an Indian encampment. It was in this area, although the exact spot is unknown, that Governor Juan de Ugalde of Coahuila, New Spain, attacked an Apache ranchería in retaliation for raids in his province. During the battle one Apache was killed and six were captured. This was a small victory compared to other battles Ugalde had launched against the Apache, but it had serious political ramifications. This area was in the province of Nueva Vizcaya, and the Apache were at peace with the local authorities.

Today the canyon is peaceful and offers a respite for the hiker. The clash of arms may have rung in the canyon in the spring of 1787, but today the melodious song of the canyon wren and the soft babble of a small creek create a soothing concert.

Depending on rainfall, surface water can often be found flowing in a narrow stream in the lower two-thirds of the canyon. Do not be fooled by this trickle. Huge, dead cottonwood logs jammed in the rocks well above the canyon floor testify that the water flow can increase tremendously in a short period of time. Be aware of surrounding storms, as a heavy rain can cause severe flash floods in the canyon.

A hiker follows Rancherías Canyon deep into the Bofecillos Mountains.

The water in the stream is quite palatable, originating in volcanic rock. However, be sure to purify it before drinking. Do not count on water always being available without asking first at Fort Leaton or the Barton Warnock Center. On day hikes it is usually easier to carry all the water needed rather than bother with purification.

Because of the usually dependable water supply, the canyon is a sensitive riparian area. Wildlife finds refuge, water, and food in the canyon, and the hiker should move quietly to disturb the many creatures as little as possible. Javelina frequent the area; let them get around you without blocking their way when necessary. Like most animals, they feel threatened when cornered in physically restricted areas like this box canyon.

At the end of the nineteenth century, mercury was discovered in the Big Bend region. To shore up mineshafts, fuel the smelters, and obtain firewood for cooking and heating, woodcutters stripped the cottonwood, willow, and ash trees lining the region's watercourses. Rancherías Canyon has good stands of cottonwoods and willows, much of it probably regrowth. Be careful not to trample the many new saplings; they represent the rebirth of the Big Bend.

Rancherías Canyon

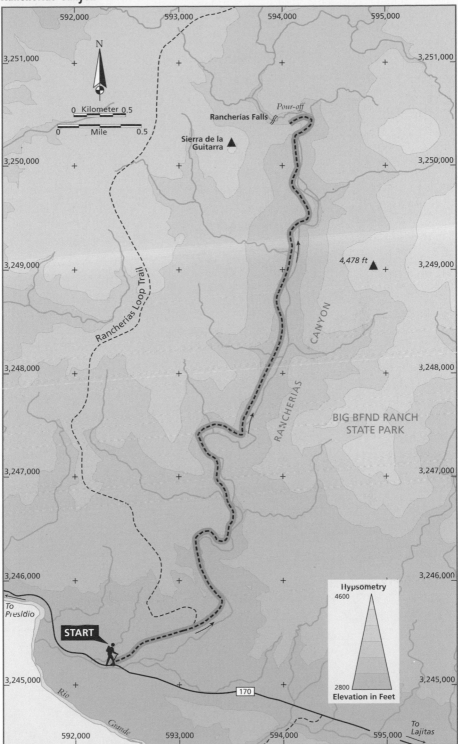

N

0 Kilometer 0.5

0 Mile 0.5

592,000   593,000   594,000   595,000

3,251,000

3,250,000

3,249,000

3,248,000

3,247,000

3,246,000

3,245,000

Pour-off

Rancherías Falls

Sierra de la
Guitarra

4,478 ft

CANYON

RANCHERÍAS

BIG BEND RANCH
STATE PARK

Rancherías Loop Trail

START

To
Presidio

Rio

Grande

170

To
Lajitas

Hypsometry
4600

2800
Elevation in Feet

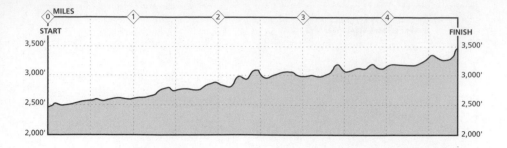

The canyon cuts through several lava flows from at least three different volcanoes. Lava flows from eruptions of the Bofecillos volcano north of the canyon and the Sierra Rica volcano to the south in Mexico make up much of the canyon walls. These two volcanoes alternately erupted several times from 28 to 26 million years ago and their deposits are interbedded in the canyon walls. An older lava flow, about 34 million years old, is also found in the canyon; it originated from the Chinati Mountains some 45 miles to the northwest. Water flowing from the Bofecillos Mountains has cut through millions of years of geologic history, exposing a time when the land was in violent upheaval.

At the end of the canyon the route climbs up a small pour-off to reach the base of Rancherías Falls, one of the highest in Texas. Its flow, or lack thereof, depends on rainfall. A clear pool at the bottom catches the water falling from the terrace above. Please keep the pool undisturbed and clean by not entering the water, however tempting it may be. Bathing is prohibited because it contaminates the water with sunscreen, body oils, and bacteria. Another reason to stay out: Leeches have been seen in the pool.

After enjoying the sounds and sights of Rancherías Falls, plan to return by the same route. Do not attempt to continue up the canyon above the falls or climb out to join the Rancherías Loop Trail to the west. Unstable rock and nearly vertical canyon walls make such climbs very dangerous. Besides, Rancherías Canyon is beautiful enough to compel a return along the same route.

Miles and Directions

0.0 Trailhead on TX FM 170.

0.75 Fork in old road. Go right, drop into canyon bottom, and follow it upstream.

4.8 Rancherías Falls.

47 Rancherías Loop

General description: A backpack through the heart of Big Bend Ranch State Park.
Distance: 19-mile loop.
Approximate hiking time: 9.5 to 10 hours.
Difficulty: Very strenuous.

Traffic: Light.
Trail surface: Dirt path.
Topo maps: Redford SE, Santana Mesa, Sauceda Ranch, Agua Adentro Mountain.

Finding the trailhead: The East Rancherías Loop trailhead parking area is marked and located on the south side of Texas Highway FM 170 about 21 miles west of the Barton Warnock Environmental Education Center near Lajitas and 29 miles east of Fort Leaton State Historical Park near Presidio. The West Rancherías Loop trailhead is marked and located on the north side of the highway 23 miles west of the Warnock Center and 27 miles east of Fort Leaton. This description starts from the eastern trailhead. Be sure to get a permit at Fort Leaton or the Warnock Center before you start.

The Hike

The Rancherías Loop Trail passes through two desert canyons, by two reliable springs, and over ridges and mesas. The terrain is very rough with some steep climbs. Other than at the trailheads, the trail is marked only by rock cairns. This a trail for experienced desert hikers in good physical condition who can read topographic maps and use a compass. Three days and two nights are recommended for the trip. When the trail is broken into three segments, the daily mileage averages 6.3 miles, considered short for many backpackers. The terrain, however, demands extra time and energy. People who have required rescue on this trail have usually gotten into trouble because they overestimated their ability and underestimated the terrain. This is not a trail for beginning desert hikers.

The Rancherías Loop Trail is not a complete loop. Both trailheads are located on Texas Highway FM 170, but are separated by 2.5 miles. To make a full loop, hikers must walk an additional 2.5 miles along the highway. Be alert for traffic; TX FM 170 is narrow with no shoulders. Hitchhiking is not advised.

It is easier to follow the trail in a counter-clockwise course, starting at the east trailhead. This route has a more gradual elevation gain and the rock cairns are easier to read traveling in this direction. Hikers beginning at the west trailhead will have to ascend approximately 1,500 feet in 3 miles with no switchbacks.

There are two major springs on the trail that have water year-round except during the driest times. Be sure to check on their status at the Barton Warnock Center or Fort Leaton before beginning hiking. The water must be treated before drinking. The trail description begins at the eastern trailhead and is divided into three segments.

Miles and Directions

0.0   East trailhead on TX FM 170.

2.2   Enter Acebuches Canyon and follow it upstream.

2.7   Seep Spring.

3.8   Junction with Cañon Santana. Follow right fork, Acebuches Canyon.

5.5   Saddle between Acebuches and Panther Canyons.

6.2   Casa Reza.

7.3   Panther Spring.

8.2   Trail joins old road and turns northwest onto it.

8.7   Dry water trough.

11.3   A side road turns right into north fork of Rancherías Canyon; stay straight and continue down main canyon.

12.3   Rancherías Spring.

13.7   North end of Lower Guale Mesa.

15.9   South end of Lower Guale Mesa.

19.0   West trailhead on TX FM 170.

Segment One

5.5 miles, 1,515-foot net elevation gain

The trail starts on the north side of the road across from the parking area and soon drops into an arroyo. As in all desert arroyos and canyons, be alert for flash floods if storms threaten. Watch for the rock cairns and follow the drainage, bearing right at each confluence. The arroyo will lead to the head of a box canyon with a rock fence. The trail then leaves the arroyo and goes through a gap in the rock fence and proceeds along the north side of a small drainage. The trail gains altitude until a divide is reached. If you began hiking before dawn, this divide provides an excellent view of the sunrise.

The trail then drops down into Acebuches Canyon; acebuches is a colloquial Spanish name for a desert tree, the netleaf hackberry. Follow the rock cairns leading up the northeast-trending canyon. Acebuches Canyon is in a fault zone within a down-dropped block of land called the Madera Graben. It is the contact zone between two volcanic events, one from the ancient Bofecillos volcano in the state park and the other from the Sierra Rica volcano across the Rio Grande in Chihuahua, Mexico. Once in the deep, sheer-walled canyon, follow it upstream along the canyon floor. A grove of cottonwoods and willows indicate a small seep spring that sometimes has water at the surface.

A yucca blooms high above Colorado Canyon. ▶

At the head of the deepest part of the canyon, you encounter a major fork. The left fork is called Cañon Santana. Cañon Santana intersects with Acebuches Canyon at the base of a 50-foot pour-off. The trail continues in the right-hand fork in Acebuches Canyon. After entering the right fork, watch for cairns that lead you out of the canyon on the left side. At this point the trail is very steep with numerous switchbacks that parallel the canyon. Walk carefully; a misstep here would be disastrous. After a hard climb of more than a mile, the trail tops out on a divide between Acebuches and Panther (Leon) Canyons. The saddle dividing the canyons is a good camping spot and the end of the first trail segment.

Segment Two

6.8 miles, 340-foot net elevation loss

Leaving the divide, the trail drops steeply into a large canyon, called Panther in English and Leon in Spanish. Both names derive from the mountain lions that live in the area. On the canyon floor is a large spring with two adobe buildings. This site is called Casa Reza, after the Reza family who homesteaded here in about 1911. The larger structure was used for sleeping, while the smaller was a kitchen. Oral tradition says that the Rezas lived in a nearby cave until they could afford to build their home complex. Casa Reza was restored in 1993 by the Texas Parks and Wildlife Department.

The Rezas cultivated a fruit orchard and vegetable crops, and raised goats for asadero cheese and wool. They sold their products in Lajitas by making long, arduous trips out of the canyon. Because water is available at the spring, many people will prefer to come here, rather than the saddle, to spend the first night on the trail. However, because of the delicate spring ecosystem and historic buildings, this is a critical management area. Camping is allowed only across the drainage from the adobe house and kitchen. Please do not alter or pick up artifacts in the vicinity, even if they look like junk.

From Casa Reza, the trail proceeds north up Panther Canyon, following the west bank. The trail then drops into the canyon bottom except to skirt boulders and pour-offs. After a rock fence the trail passes a boulder called La Fecha ("The Date"), marked with an inscription dated 1934.

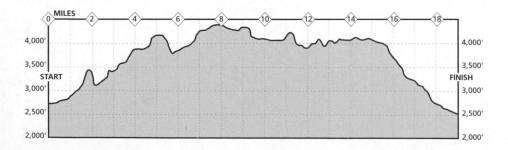

Rancherías Loop

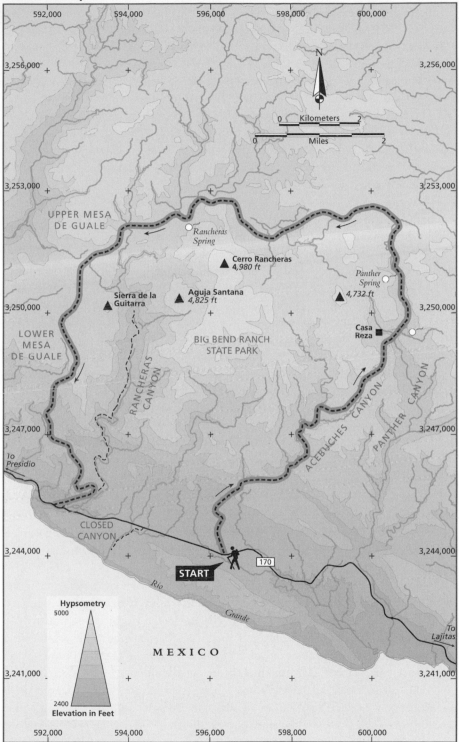

592,000 594,000 596,000 598,000 600,000

3,256,000

N

0   Kilometers   2

0   Miles   2

3,253,000

UPPER MESA
DE GUALE

Rancheras
Spring

Cerro Rancheras
4,980 ft

Panther
Spring

Sierra de la
Guitarra

Aguja Santana
4,825 ft

4,732 ft

3,250,000

Casa
Reza

LOWER
MESA
DE GUALE

BIG BEND RANCH
STATE PARK

RANCHERAS CANYON

ACEBUCHES CANYON

PANTHER CANYON

3,247,000

To
Presidio

CLOSED
CANYON

START   170

3,244,000

Rio

Grande

To
Lajitas

Hypsometry

5000

MEXICO

2400
Elevation in Feet

3,241,000

592,000 594,000 596,000 598,000 600,000

Farther up the canyon, the trail passes Panther Spring in a side canyon on the left, marked by lush vegetation and trees. Water piped from the spring once filled a trough here. Maps available from the Texas Parks and Wildlife Department show several water troughs along the trail. These are shown for landmark purposes only and no longer have water. Because the spring flows through such a small, narrow area, it could be trampled and damaged by people using it. Please do not enter the spring area.

The trail continues through a barbed wire fence and then makes a steep climb, skirting some difficult areas in the canyon bottom. It then drops back into the canyon bottom just downstream from a shelter cave found on the right-hand side of the canyon. Prehistoric Indians and Hispanic pastores, or goatherders, once occupied the cave. Please do not disturb this site.

Continue to follow rock cairns north toward the head of the canyon. The trail continues to leave and re-enter the drainage to avoid obstacles. As the drainage climbs, the canyon walls fall away and the trail enters more open country.

The drainage soon intersects an old dirt road. Look for a series of cairns turning the trail sharply left, or northwest, onto the old road. Do not follow the northeast-bound road, as this will take you far off the proper route. The old road followed by the trail was once an important route between Lajitas and Redford. About 0.5 mile along this road there will be a dry water trough lying to the south.

A mountain, Cerro Rancherías, dominates the skyline to the southwest as you continue west on the old road. To the northwest is a rugged peak called Aguja de la Colmena, or Honeybee Peak. Slightly west and beyond is Oso Peak, the highest point in Big Bend Ranch State Park at 5,135 feet. The trail enters a broad valley, the upper reaches of the east fork of Rancherías Canyon, and crosses an eroded dome formed by magma cooling under the surface 20 to 30 million years ago. Along the road are outcroppings of Boquillas Limestone, perhaps 90 million years old. The older limestone was thrust upward by underground igneous activity. This is one of the few places in the Bofecillos Mountains where limestone is exposed.

Another road will join from the north, entering from the north fork of Rancherías Canyon; follow the cairns and continue west along the road you have been traveling. Sierra de la Guitarra will appear to the south down the main canyon. A long ridge extending south from the main summit gives it the appearance of a guitar and its Spanish name.

A large grove of trees marks Rancherías Spring, the second major water source on the trail and the end of the second trail segment. Rancherías Spring is the water source for the falls in Rancherías Canyon. Because it is a major spring in the Bofecillos Mountains and a delicate riparian area, it has been designated a critical management zone. Please do not enter the fragile area shown on the maps issued by the Texas Parks and Wildlife Department and obtained with your hiking permit.

Sanitation is important, but only one of the reasons for camping at least 300 feet from a water source. The Apaches would not camp in such areas because they believed they did not own the springs. Wildlife must be able to use these water sources, but may not be able to if people are nearby. To protect wildlife, the Texas Parks and Wildlife Department has continued the Apache philosophy. Springs are just as important for wildlife today as they were hundreds of years ago.

Segment Three

6.7 miles, 1,400-foot net elevation loss

The trail leaves Rancherías Spring along a part of a historic pack trail between Lajitas and Redford that was known as Muerte del Burro ("Death of the Donkey"). It starts with a good climb out of the main Rancherías drainage, drops into a tributary of Rancherías Canyon, and climbs out again across broken terrain, crossing washes and ridges to the west. The yellow cliffs ahead are bluffs dividing the upper and lower portions of Mesa de Guale. This is often miscalled "Wylie Mesa." The name Guale (pronounced WALL-eh) is a nickname for a man named Guadalupe Carrasco, whose descendants still live in the area.

As the trail drops onto Lower Mesa de Guale, it joins a historic north–south wagon road that was built by the Fowlkes brothers when they were ranching the mesa. The rock work attests to the determination that settlers of the Big Bend region have always exhibited. In places there are grooves worn deep into solid rock where wagon wheels were locked or sledge runners cut into the stone while going down steep inclines.

The trail grade flattens while crossing Lower Mesa de Guale. The canyon to the west bounding Mesa de Guale is popularly called Tapado Canyon. Tapado means "covered"; the canyon is blocked with boulders. An older name for this canyon is Oso Canyon, meaning "black bear," for the animals that once inhabited the area. There are numerous side trails in this area, but many lead into private land. Be sure to stay on the marked trail.

The trail passes Sierra de la Guitarra on its west side, giving a dramatic view of this peak. At the southern end of the mesa is a dry concrete trough with the name Cryspin Reza inscribed in it. Reza, who was related to the Reza family of Panther Canyon, was a master stone worker who oversaw the construction of many such troughs and water tanks on Big Bend Ranch.

Where the trail drops off of Mesa de Guale, stop and look out over the broad sweep of country. In the southern distance, the majestic Sierra Ricas of Mexico rise over 8,000 feet high. This extinct volcano was responsible for much of the igneous deposits you have been hiking through. Silver, lead, and zinc were mined from this range until the mid-1940s. The Rio Grande forms a narrow green belt below until it ducks out of sight in Colorado Canyon. Colorado Mesa forms the north wall of the canyon, and it dominates the foreground. Looking down on top of Colorado Mesa, the narrow chasm of Closed Canyon draining into the river can be seen.

At this overlook, a microcosm of the Chihuahuan Desert divided by two nations is displayed. Look on both sides of the river—little difference can be seen. Dead volcanoes now separated by the Rio Grande were equally responsible for this stunning landscape. Political boundaries divide the ecosystem, but events on one side affect the other. The edge of Mesa de Guale is a place for inspiration.

From the mesa, the trail drops steeply 1,500 feet in about 3 miles. Historians believe that wagons traveling this road did so only downhill and another gentler climb was used to return to the ranch. Watch your footing as you descend the steep grade. The trail terminates at the parking area for the West Rancherías trailhead.

Suggested Reading

National Park Service. *Big Bend*. Washington, D.C.: National Park Service, 1983.

Ragsdale, Kenneth Baxter. *Quicksilver: Terlingua and the Chisos Mining Company*. College Station, Texas: Texas A & M University Press, 1976.

Tyler, Ronnie C. *The Big Bend: A History of the Last Texas Frontier*. Washington, D.C.: National Park Service, 1975.

Wuerthner, George. *Texas' Big Bend Country*. Helena, Montana: American Geographic Publishing, 1989.

About the Author

Laurence Parent was born and raised in New Mexico. After receiving an engineering degree at the University of Texas at Austin, he practiced engineering for six years before becoming a full-time freelance photographer and writer specializing in landscape, travel, and nature subjects. His photos appear in Sierra Club, Audubon, and many other calendars. Article and photo credits include *National Geographic Traveler, Outside, Backpacker, Sierra,* and the *New York Times.* He contributes regularly to regional publications such as *Texas Highways, Texas Monthly, New Mexico Magazine,* and *Texas Parks & Wildlife.* Other work includes posters, advertising, museum exhibits, postcards, and brochures.

Parent has completed twenty-nine books, including six other guidebooks for Falcon: *Hiking New Mexico, Hiking Texas, Scenic Driving New Mexico, Scenic Driving Wyoming, Scenic Driving North Carolina,* and *Scenic Driving Texas.* His latest work is *Lighthouses: Sentinels of the American Coast,* a large-format, coffee-table book produced by Graphic Arts Center Publishing. He makes his home near Austin, Texas, with his wife Patricia.

WHAT'S SO SPECIAL ABOUT UNSPOILED, NATURAL PLACES?

Beauty   Solitude   Wildness   Freedom   Quiet   Adventure
Serenity   Inspiration   Wonder   Excitement
Relaxation   Challenge

There's a lot to love about our treasured public lands, and the reasons are different for each of us. Whatever your reasons are, the national **Leave No Trace** education program will help you discover special outdoor places, enjoy them, and preserve them—today and for those who follow. By practicing and passing along these simple principles, you can help protect the special places you love from being loved to death.

THE PRINCIPLES OF **LEAVE NO TRACE**

- Plan ahead and prepare
- Travel and camp on durable surfaces
- Dispose of waste properly
- Leave what you find
- Minimize campfire impacts
- Respect wildlife
- Be considerate of other visitors

Leave No Trace is a national nonprofit organization dedicated to teaching responsible outdoor recreation skills and ethics to everyone who enjoys spending time outdoors.

To learn more or to become a member, please visit us at www.LNT.org or call (800) 332-4100.

Leave No Trace, P.O. Box 997, Boulder, CO 80306